delicious. MAGAZINE
EVERYDAY SUPPERS

Edited by Debbie Major

Magazine Editor
Matthew Drennan

HarperCollins*Publishers*

contents

introduction   6

conversion tables   8

pasta, noodles, rice and other grains   10
meat   40
chicken and poultry   68
fish and shellfish   96
meat-free suppers   126
cheese and eggs   154

additional tips   182

index and acknowledgements   188

introduction

What shall I cook for supper tonight? The question often crops up on a daily basis – and this book will solve that dilemma every time. What I love most about *Everyday Suppers* is that first it offers anyone who knows and loves good food some brilliant new ideas for weeknight meals, and secondly, it will inspire the less adventurous cook to try new dishes that are easy to prepare and cook. These simple suppers form the backbone of each issue of **delicious.** magazine, offering readers new inspiration every month.

The book is divided into chapters covering pasta and rice; meat; chicken; fish and meat-free dishes; and cheese and eggs, making it easy for you to choose what you want to eat. As time is of the essence to all of us, you will also find many speedy suppers such as beef and bok choi noodles, grilled pork chops rarebit-style or chicken and chorizo pilaff. There are also lots of clever family meals that won't break the bank, such as cauliflower and macaroni cheese, creamy pancetta, brie and mushroom croissants and spaghetti with avocado pesto.

One of my favourite chapters is cheese and eggs because it offers up clever recipes such as cheese and thyme soufflés and oozy mushroom omelettes that use everyday ingredients you're likely to have in your fridge, storecupboard or freezer.

Everyday Suppers is packed with meals everyone will love and a handy shopping checklist at the back of the book, plus hints and tips on how to take the stress out of cooking every day.

Matthew Drennan
delicious. Magazine Editor

Conversion tables

All the recipes in this book list only metric measurements (also used by Australian cooks). The conversions listed here are approximate for imperial measurements (also used by American cooks).

Oven temperatures

°C	Fan°C	°F	Gas	Description
110	90	225	¼	Very cool
120	100	250	½	Very cool
140	120	275	1	Cool
150	130	300	2	Cool
160	140	325	3	Warm
180	160	350	4	Moderate
190	170	375	5	Moderately hot
200	180	400	6	Fairly hot
220	200	425	7	Hot
230	210	450	8	Very hot
240	220	475	9	Very hot

Weights for dry ingredients

Metric	Imperial	Metric	Imperial
7g	¼oz	425g	15oz
15g	½oz	450g	1lb
20g	¾oz	500g	1lb 2oz
25g	1oz	550g	1¼lb
40g	1½oz	600g	1lb 5oz
50g	2oz	650g	1lb 7oz
60g	2½oz	675g	1½lb
75g	3oz	700g	1lb 9oz
100g	3½oz	750g	1lb 11oz
125g	4oz	800g	1¾lb
140g	4½oz	900g	2lb
150g	5oz	1kg	2¼lb
165g	5½oz	1.1kg	2½lb
175g	6oz	1.25kg	2¾lb
200g	7oz	1.35kg	3lb
225g	8oz	1.5kg	3lb 6oz
250g	9oz	1.8kg	4lb
275g	10oz	2kg	4½lb
300g	11oz	2.25kg	5lb
350g	12oz	2.5kg	5½lb
375g	13oz	2.75kg	6lb
400g	14oz	3kg	6¾lb

Liquid measures

Metric	Imperial	Aus	US
25ml	1fl oz		
50ml	2fl oz	¼ cup	¼ cup
75ml	3fl oz		
100ml	3½fl oz		
120ml	4fl oz	½ cup	½ cup
150ml	5fl oz		
175ml	6 fl oz	¾ cup	¾ cup
200ml	7fl oz		
250ml	8fl oz	1 cup	1 cup
300ml	10fl oz/½ pint	½ pint	1¼ cups
360ml	12fl oz		
400ml	14fl oz		
450ml	15fl oz	2 cups	2 cups/1 pint
600ml	1 pint	1 pint	2½ cups
750ml	1¼ pints		
900ml	1½ pints		
1 litre	1¾ pints	1¾ pints	1 quart
1.2 litres	2 pints		
1.4 litres	2½ pints		
1.5 litres	2¾ pints		
1.7 litres	3 pints		
2 litres	3½ pints		
3 litres	5¼ pints		

UK–Australian tablespoon conversions

1 x UK or Australian teaspoon is 5ml

1 x UK tablespoon is 3 teaspoons/15ml

1 Australian tablespoon is 4 teaspoons/20ml

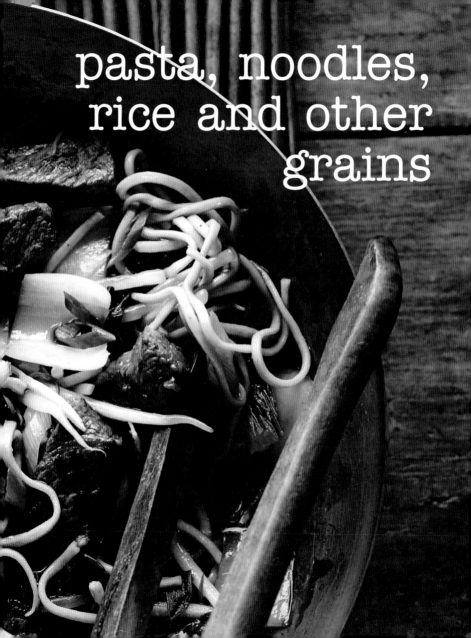

pasta, noodles, rice and other grains

Roasted artichoke and pancetta pasta

Orzo is a small pasta shape that looks like large grains of rice. If you can't get orzo, any small pasta shape will work here.

SERVES 4
READY IN 20 MINUTES

350g orzo or any small pasta shapes

70g piece pancetta, cut into small strips

100g roasted artichokes in olive oil, drained and halved

4 tbsp fresh pesto

50g wild rocket leaves

1. Cook the orzo in a large pan of boiling water, according to the packet instructions.

2. Meanwhile, fry the pancetta in a non-stick pan for a few minutes, until golden and crispy, then remove and drain on kitchen paper.

3. Drain the orzo, reserving the cooking water. Return the orzo to the pan along with 2 tablespoons of the cooking water. Add the pancetta, artichokes, pesto and rocket leaves, toss together well and serve immediately.

Lamb biryani

This classic Indian dish is best when served with extra yogurt,
Indian pickles and warm naan bread.

SERVES 6

TAKES 55 MINUTES, PLUS
30–35 MINUTES IN THE OVEN,
PLUS OVERNIGHT MARINATING

250ml natural yogurt

1 green chilli, seeded and
  finely sliced

4 garlic cloves, crushed

50g piece fresh root ginger,
  grated

½ tsp each ground cloves and
  ground cinnamon

2 tsp each ground cumin and
  ground coriander

750g lamb leg steaks, trimmed
  of excess fat and cut into
  bite-sized pieces

350g basmati rice

100ml milk

1 tsp ground saffron

2 large onions, finely sliced

75g ghee or melted butter,
  plus 1 extra tbsp

1 long cinnamon stick, broken
  into 3 pieces

12 cardamom pods, cracked

Crispy onions and chopped
  fresh coriander, to garnish

1. Mix the yogurt, chilli, garlic, ginger, cloves,
cinnamon, half the ground cumin and coriander,
lamb and seasoning in a bowl. Cover and
chill overnight.

2. The next day, remove the lamb from fridge.
Rinse the rice and soak in cold water for
30 minutes. While the rice is soaking, heat the
milk, add the saffron, and set aside.

3. Meanwhile, preheat the oven to 150°C/
fan 130°C/gas 2. In a wide-based pan, cook the
onions in the 75g of ghee or butter for 15 minutes,
until golden. Add the remaining ground cumin and
coriander, cook for 1 minute and set aside.

4. Drain the rice. Bring some water, the cinnamon
stick, cardamom pods and salt to the boil in a pan.
Add the rice and boil for 2 minutes. Drain and mix
into the onions.

5. Melt 1 tablespoon of ghee or butter in a large
flameproof casserole dish over a low heat. Spoon
in one-third of the rice and top with half the lamb.
Repeat once more, drizzling over half the saffron
milk. Cover with the remaining rice and saffron
milk. Cover with foil and a lid, heat for 30 seconds,
then bake for 30–35 minutes until the lamb is
tender. Sprinkle with the crispy onions and fresh
coriander and serve.

Spaghetti with prawns, lemon, chilli, garlic and rocket

A quick, light pasta dish that's easy to make and even easier to enjoy.

SERVES 4
READY IN 20 MINUTES

400g dried spaghetti

6 tbsp olive oil

3 garlic cloves, crushed

2 medium–hot red chillies, seeded and finely chopped

150g vine-ripened tomatoes, skinned and chopped

Finely grated zest of ½ lemon, plus 2 tbsp fresh lemon juice

300–400g cooked peeled tiger prawns, thawed if frozen

150g rocket leaves

1. Bring a large saucepan of water to the boil. Add the spaghetti and cook according to the packet instructions or until the pasta is al dente.

2. Shortly before the spaghetti is ready, put the oil and garlic into a large, deep frying pan over a medium heat. As soon as the garlic starts to sizzle, add the chillies and fry for 1 minute. Add the tomatoes and fry for a further minute. Add the lemon zest, lemon juice, prawns and some seasoning, and cook for 1½–2 minutes, until the prawns are heated through.

3. Drain the spaghetti and add to the pan of prawns along with the rocket, and toss together well. Divide among four warmed pasta bowls and serve.

Paella-style dirty rice

In New Orleans, they serve 'dirty rice' with just about everything.
Here's a good veggie version made with kidney beans.

SERVES 4
READY IN 50 MINUTES

350g long grain rice
2 tbsp ground cumin
2 litres vegetable stock, hot
1 tbsp vegetable oil
1 onion, sliced
2 garlic cloves, crushed
3 celery sticks, chopped
2 x 400g cans kidney beans
  in water, drained and rinsed
Small handful of chopped
  fresh coriander
2 handfuls of baby leaf spinach
150g okra, blanched
1 tbsp chopped fresh thyme
Pinch of smoked paprika
Hot Jamaican sauce and
  soft-boiled eggs, to serve
  (optional)

1. Put the rice, cumin and stock in a large saucepan over a high heat. Bring to the boil, then reduce the heat slightly and simmer for 15 minutes or until the rice is just cooked and most of the stock has been absorbed.

2. Meanwhile, heat the oil in a large frying pan over a medium heat. Add the onion, garlic and celery, and cook, stirring occasionally, for 6–8 minutes, until the vegetables are soft but not coloured.

3. Take the cooked rice off the heat, add the onion mixture and all the remaining ingredients, and mix together well. Season to taste.

4. Divide the 'dirty rice' among serving plates and serve with a hot Jamaican sauce and soft-boiled eggs, if you like.

Macaroni, pancetta and basil frittata

A frittata makes a lovely light supper. You can use 150g of leftover cooked pasta instead of the macaroni, if you prefer.

SERVES 4
READY IN 45 MINUTES

75g dried macaroni
75g diced pancetta
1 garlic clove, finely chopped
5 large eggs
75g Parmesan or Grana
  Padano, roughly chopped
Large handful of fresh basil
  leaves, plus extra to serve
Dressed mixed salad, to serve

1. Cook the macaroni in a large pan of boiling salted water according to the packet instructions, then drain well and set aside to cool a little.

2. Sizzle the pancetta in a 20cm non-stick, ovenproof frying pan for 3–4 minutes, until it begins to crisp up. Add the garlic and cook for 30 seconds more. Remove from the heat and set aside.

3. Meanwhile, crack the eggs into a large bowl and beat together well. Remove the pancetta from the pan with a slotted spoon, then stir it into the eggs along with the cooked macaroni, the cheese, basil leaves and some black pepper.

4. Put the frying pan back over a medium heat. Pour in the frittata mixture and cook for 8–10 minutes, until almost set. Meanwhile, preheat the grill to Medium.

5. Place the pan under the grill for 4–5 minutes, until the frittata is golden brown and set.

6. Leave to sit in the pan for 5 minutes, then slide on to a chopping board. Cut into wedges and serve warm or at room temperature. Garnish with extra basil leaves and serve with a dressed mixed salad.

Variation You can slip almost anything you fancy into a frittata. Try adding some blanched peas and mint, or make it with some roasted red pepper strips, crumbled feta and drained, roasted artichokes from a jar.

Butternut squash and creamy blue cheese risotto

This is real comfort food on its own, but it's even better with grilled portobello mushrooms flavoured with thyme and olive oil.

SERVES 4
READY IN 1 HOUR

1 large onion, finely chopped
2 bay leaves
2 large fresh thyme sprigs
500g butternut squash, peeled, seeded and cut into small pieces
3 tbsp olive oil
15–20 fresh sage leaves
350g arborio rice
150ml dry fruity white wine, such as Pinot Grigio
125g creamy blue cheese, such as dolcelatte, crumbled

1. Bring 1.25 litres of water to the boil in a large pan. Add half the onion, the bay leaves, thyme, squash and some salt, and cook for 10 minutes until soft. Drain well, reserving the liquid as a stock. Purée the squash and onion with 2 tablespoons of the stock, until smooth. Bring the remaining stock to the boil, and keep hot.

2. Heat 1 tablespoon of oil in a heavy-based pan. Fry the sage leaves briefly, then drain on kitchen paper.

3. Add the rest of the oil and onion to the pan, and cook gently for 10 minutes, until soft but not coloured. Add the rice, then the wine and cook for 2 minutes.

4. Add the stock a ladleful at a time, stirring until it has been absorbed before adding another. After about 20 minutes, all the stock will have been absorbed and the rice will creamy and tender. Add the squash purée and stir until hot. Stir in two-thirds of the cheese, ladle into warm bowls, and scatter over the remaining cheese and crisp sage leaves.

Variation If you are not a fan of blue cheese, try stirring in some creamy fresh goat's cheese and a handful of grated Parmesan instead.

Spaghetti with avocado pesto

This summer dish is at its best when enjoyed al fresco.

SERVES 4
READY IN 20 MINUTES

450g dried spaghetti
1 slightly under-ripe avocado
Juice of ½ lemon
15g packet fresh basil, roughly torn
1 garlic clove, roughly chopped
6 tbsp olive oil
1 red chilli, seeded and very finely chopped
40g Parmesan, grated, plus shavings to serve

1. Bring a large pan of salted water to the boil. Add the spaghetti and cook according to the packet instructions or until al dente.

2. Meanwhile, make the avocado pesto. Halve and stone the avocado, scoop out the flesh and put it into a food processor. Add the lemon juice, torn basil, chopped garlic and olive oil, and pulse briefly to make a rough-textured, pesto-like sauce. Stir in the red chilli and grated Parmesan, then season to taste.

3. Drain the spaghetti, stir in the avocado pesto and check the seasoning. Divide among four warm bowls and top with some Parmesan shavings to serve.

Five spice duck and ginger noodle soup

This tasty dish is packed with healthy ingredients and vibrant Asian flavours. It's also great if you're watching your waistline.

SERVES 4
READY IN 35 MINUTES

Pinch of crushed dried chillies

¼ tsp Chinese five spice powder

½ tsp sugar

2 large duck breasts, skin removed

2 litres fresh chicken stock, hot

5cm piece fresh root ginger, cut into thin strips

2 tsp sunflower oil

200g dried wholewheat noodles

1 medium–hot red chilli, seeded and thinly sliced

Bunch of spring onions, trimmed and thinly sliced on the diagonal

200g beansprouts

4 pak choi heads, roughly chopped

Handful of fresh coriander sprigs

Dark soy sauce, to serve

1. Grind the crushed chillies in a pestle and mortar, then mix in a shallow dish with the five spice powder, sugar, salt and some pepper. Put the duck breasts skinned-side down on the spices. Cover with a plate and weigh down. Set aside for 10 minutes.

2. Meanwhile, bring the stock and ginger to the boil in a pan. Season lightly and keep hot. Bring another pan of lightly salted water to the boil for the noodles.

3. Heat the sunflower oil in a frying pan over a medium–high heat. Add the duck breasts, spice-side down, lower the heat slightly and cook for 3 minutes each side for medium–rare. Set aside to rest for 5 minutes.

4. Cook the noodles in the boiling water according to the packet instructions. Drain and divide among four warm bowls. Sprinkle with the chilli and half the spring onions. Add the beansprouts and pak choi to the chicken stock and cook for 1 minute. Ladle over the noodles.

5. Thinly slice the duck and place on top. Scatter with the remaining spring onions and coriander sprigs, and serve with the dark soy sauce.

Easy prawn laksa

Laksa is a spicy paste made from garlic, lemongrass, chilli and almonds. Use it to make this exciting Asian noodle soup with a real kick.

SERVES 4
READY IN 1 HOUR

20 raw prawns, shells and heads on
3 tbsp vegetable oil
400ml can coconut milk
Juice of 2 limes
1 tsp sugar
2 tbsp Thai fish sauce
200g dried medium egg noodles
¼ cucumber, cut into thin strips, to serve
Small bunch of fresh coriander, to serve

For the laksa paste:

2 medium–hot red chillies, seeded if you prefer
2 garlic cloves, roughly chopped
2.5cm piece fresh root ginger or galangal, roughly chopped
4 small shallots, roughly chopped
1 lemongrass stick, outer layer discarded, roughly chopped
1 tbsp Thai fish sauce
50g ground almonds

1. Make the laksa paste by blitzing all the ingredients into a rough-textured paste using a mini food processor. Set aside 3 tablespoons of the paste and keep the rest in the fridge for up to 2 weeks, or freeze it.

2. Remove the heads and peel the prawns, leaving the last tail segment in place. Pop the heads and shells into a pan with 750ml cold water, and simmer for 30 minutes. Strain the stock into a jug, discarding the solids.

3. Heat the oil in a large pan or wok over a medium heat. Add the prawns and fry for 2 minutes. Add the laksa paste and fry for 2 minutes more. Add the coconut milk, lime juice, sugar, fish sauce and shellfish stock, and bring to a gentle simmer.

4. Cook the noodles in boiling water according to the packet instructions, then drain and divide among four bowls. Top with the prawns and their soup, then garnish with the cucumber and coriander to serve.

DELICIOUS. TIP If you don't want to make your own laksa paste, you can buy it from major supermarkets or just use a good Thai red curry paste instead.

Prawn and chorizo jambalaya

This spicy, zingy Creole dish with juicy prawns is sure to become a firm family favourite.

SERVES 4
TAKES 30 MINUTES, PLUS COOLING

150g piece chorizo, diced

200g raw tiger prawns, peeled and deveined

1 small red pepper, seeded

1 small yellow pepper, seeded

1 onion, finely sliced

2 celery sticks, finely sliced on the diagonal

2 garlic cloves, crushed

1 medium–hot red chilli, seeded and finely chopped

Leaves from a few fresh thyme sprigs

200g long grain rice

227g can chopped tomatoes

700ml vegetable or chicken stock, hot

½ tsp Tabasco sauce, plus extra to serve

4 spring onions, trimmed and finely sliced

Lime wedges, to serve

1. Stir-fry the chorizo and prawns in a wide, deep frying pan over a medium–high heat, stirring occasionally for 3–4 minutes until the prawns are just cooked through and the chorizo is lightly golden. Remove with a slotted spoon to a plate, cover and set aside.

2. Slice the peppers and add them to the pan with the onion, celery, garlic and chilli, and cook, stirring occasionally for 5 minutes, until softened slightly. Stir in the thyme and rice, cook for 1 minute, then add the tomatoes, stock and Tabasco, and bring to the boil. Cover, reduce the heat to low and simmer very gently, stirring occasionally, for 12 minutes, until most of the liquid has evaporated. Season to taste.

3. Stir in the chorizo, prawns and spring onions, and cook for 2–3 minutes until heated through. Serve with the lime wedges and extra Tabasco sauce.

Variation You could swap the prawns for diced, skinned chicken breasts. Stir-fry with the chorizo in step 1, as above, until just cooked.

Beef and bok choi noodles

Not only low in calories, this Chinese-inspired dish is also
quick, simple, healthy and filling.

SERVES 4
READY IN 15 MINUTES

225g dried medium egg
  noodles

300g lean beef steak, such as
  sirloin or fillet, trimmed of
  all fat

1 tbsp light soy sauce

1 tbsp oyster sauce

2 tbsp Chinese rice wine

2 tsp rice wine vinegar

1 tsp sunflower oil

5cm piece fresh root ginger,
  cut into fine matchsticks

4 small bok choi heads, cut
  into wide strips

Bunch of spring onions,
  trimmed and cut on the
  diagonal into 1cm slices

100g fresh beansprouts

1 tsp toasted sesame oil

1. Bring a large pan of lightly salted water to the
boil. Add the noodles and cook for 4 minutes, until
just tender. Drain and set aside.

2. Cut the steak into thin slices, about 2cm wide.
Spread out on a plate and season. In a small bowl,
mix together the soy sauce, oyster sauce, rice wine
and vinegar. Set aside.

3. Heat the oil in a wok or large, deep, non-stick
frying pan over a high heat. Add the steak and
stir-fry for 1 minute, until just cooked. Lift out with
a slotted spoon and set aside. Add the ginger, bok
choi, spring onions and beansprouts. Stir-fry for
1 minute.

4. Return the beef to the pan along with the
noodles, soy and oyster sauce mixture and the
toasted sesame oil. Briefly toss together, until
heated through. Serve in warmed shallow bowls.

Variation Ring the changes by making this
dish with pork or chicken instead of beef.
You can also use pak choi or purple
sprouting broccoli instead of bok choi.

Tuscan sausage and porcini sauce with gnocchi

Simple, rustic and fantastically rich, this easy recipe is what real Italian cooking is all about.

SERVES 4
READY IN 50 MINUTES

600g good-quality pork
  sausages
25g dried porcini mushrooms
1 tbsp olive oil
50g butter
1 onion, finely chopped
250g chestnut mushrooms,
  sliced
4 garlic cloves, chopped
1 tbsp chopped fresh rosemary
200g can chopped tomatoes
4 tbsp double cream
800g gnocchi
50g shaved Parmesan,
  to serve

1. Skin the sausages and set the meat aside. Cover the porcini mushrooms with 400ml hot water and leave them to soak.

2. Heat the olive oil in a deep frying pan over a medium–high heat. Add the sausage and cook for 5 minutes, breaking it up into chunky pieces with a wooden spoon as it browns. Lift out and set aside.

3. Add the butter and the onion to the pan, and cook them gently for 5–6 minutes, stirring, until softened.

4. Drain the porcini mushrooms, reserving the liquid, and chop. Add to the onion with the chestnut mushrooms and cook for 3 minutes.

5. Return the sausage to the pan, add the garlic and rosemary, and cook for 2 minutes. Add the tomatoes and all but the last tablespoon of the mushroom liquid. Simmer for 20–25 minutes until thickened. Stir in the cream and season.

6. Cook the gnocchi in a pan of boiling salted water for 3 minutes. Drain well and divide among warmed bowls. Spoon over the sauce and scatter with Parmesan to serve.

Spring vegetable couscous

This wonderfully light and perky dish is similar to Italian minestrone but is actually based on an old Moroccan recipe.

SERVES 4
READY IN 35 MINUTES

3 tbsp olive oil

4 garlic cloves, finely sliced

1 bunch of baby turnips, about 500g, roots and tops separated

1 tsp salt

400g can flageolet or cannellini beans

2 tsp tomato purée

2 tbsp sour grape juice or white wine vinegar

1 tbsp chopped fresh dill

Generous pinch of saffron

300ml water or stock of your choice

8 young carrots, trimmed, scrubbed and halved lengthways

4 sprue (thin) asparagus spears, cut into 3–4cm pieces

1 bunch of spring onions, sliced

200g couscous

1 tbsp softened butter

1. Gently heat the oil in a large, wide saucepan, ideally with a lid. Add the garlic and cook until translucent. Add the turnip roots and salt. Stir, then reduce the heat to low, cover and leave to sweat for a good 10–15 minutes, stirring occasionally.

2. Stir in the beans, plus all the liquid from the can. Simmer, then add the tomato purée, grape juice or vinegar, dill, saffron and water or stock. Simmer until the turnips are tender. Add the carrots, asparagus and spring onions, and simmer for a few minutes until tender.

3. Meanwhile, put the couscous in a bowl and pour over 400ml boiling water, cover and leave for 5 minutes or according to the packet instructions. Fluff up with a fork, then season well and stir in the butter.

4. Remove the vegetables from the heat. Fold in the turnip tops and season. Spoon the couscous into serving bowls and ladle over the vegetables and stock.

Pearl barley risotto with roasted squash, red peppers and rocket

This comforting vegetarian risotto uses pearl barley instead of rice, giving it a beautifully nutty texture.

SERVES 4
READY IN ABOUT 1 HOUR

450g peeled butternut squash, cut into 2cm chunks

2 red peppers, halved, seeded and cut into chunky pieces

2 tbsp extra-virgin olive oil

1 medium onion, finely chopped

2 garlic cloves, finely chopped

Leaves from 3 large fresh thyme sprigs

350g pearl barley

1.5 litres vegetable stock, hot

3 tbsp chopped fresh flatleaf parsley

4 small handfuls of wild rocket and Parmesan shavings, to garnish

1. Preheat the oven to 200°C/fan 180°C/gas 6. Put the squash and peppers in a small roasting tin, drizzle with 1 tablespoon of the oil, season and toss. Roast for 35 minutes or until tender, turning halfway, then remove from the oven and set aside.

2. Meanwhile, start the risotto. Heat the remaining oil in a pan over a medium–low heat. Add the onion, garlic and thyme leaves, and cook gently, stirring occasionally for 6–8 minutes, until softened. Add the pearl barley and cook for 1 minute.

3. Add a quarter of the stock to the pan and simmer, stirring occasionally, until all the stock has been absorbed. Add another quarter of the stock and continue in this way until all the stock is absorbed – it should take about 40 minutes for the barley to be tender but still al dente.

4. Stir in the parsley, squash and peppers. Season and spoon into warmed bowls. Serve topped with the rocket and some Parmesan shavings.

meat

Grilled pork chops rarebit-style

Pork chops can be a little dry if overcooked, but using ones with the bone in will keep them moist during cooking.

SERVES 4
READY IN ABOUT 20 MINUTES

4 large pork loin chops,
  preferably with bone in and
  skin, but not the fat, removed
65g Gruyère or Emmental
  cheese, finely grated
1 tbsp Dijon mustard
3 tbsp double cream
Mashed potatoes and
  watercress salad, to serve

1. Preheat the grill to High. Snip the fat along the edge of each pork chop with scissors and discard. Season the pork chops on both sides and place them on the rack of the grill pan. Cook for 1 minute, then reduce the heat to medium–high and cook for a further 8–9 minutes. Turn the pork chops, and repeat on the other side until just cooked through.

2. Meanwhile, mix the Gruyère or Emmental with the Dijon mustard, cream and a little salt and freshly ground black pepper until it makes a thick but spreadable paste. Remove the pork chops from under the grill and turn the heat back up to high.

3. Spread the cheesy mixture over each chop and return them to the grill for 1 minute, or until the cheese is golden and bubbling. Serve with some mashed potatoes and plenty of watercress salad.

Farmer's mince

This simple recipe for farmer's mince is a variation of shepherd's pie, but with the mouthwatering addition of Parmesan and parsnips to the potato topping.

SERVES 6
TAKES 1 HOUR, PLUS
25–30 MINUTES IN THE OVEN

500g lamb mince
2 onions, finely chopped
3 carrots, finely chopped
½ swede, finely chopped
250g mushrooms, finely
   chopped
2 tbsp plain flour
2 lamb stock cubes, crumbled
2 tbsp Worcestershire sauce
2 tbsp tomato purée

For the topping:

1kg potatoes, peeled and
   cut into chunks
500g parsnips, peeled and
   cut into chunks
100ml milk
50g butter
50g Parmesan, grated

1. Heat a deep, wide frying pan over a medium–high heat. Add the lamb mince and onions, and fry for 5 minutes, until lightly browned. Add the remaining vegetables, fry for another 5 minutes, then sprinkle over the flour and crumbled stock cubes. Cook for 1 minute, then pour in 600ml boiling water and stir to combine. Add the Worcestershire sauce and tomato purée, and season. Simmer for 40 minutes.

2. Preheat the oven to 220°C/ fan 200°C/gas 7. Meanwhile, make the topping. Put the potatoes into a large pan of lightly salted water, bring to the boil and cook for 7 minutes. Add the parsnips and cook until both are tender. Drain well, then mash with the milk, butter and Parmesan. Season.

3. Spoon the mince into 4 individual ovenproof dishes and spread the mash on top with a fork. Bake for 25–30 minutes, until piping hot and golden.

Grilled gammon steaks with caramelised black pepper pineapple

This is tasty served with boiled potatoes tossed in butter, and either steamed spinach, Swiss chard, or a watercress salad.

SERVES 4
READY IN 40 MINUTES

4 x 150g gammon steaks, cut 1cm thick

1 medium-sized pineapple, about 1kg

175g caster sugar, plus

4 extra heaped tsp

25g butter, melted

½ tsp black peppercorns, coarsely crushed

1. Snip into the fatty edge of each gammon steak with scissors. Peel the pineapple and cut across into 1cm-thick slices. Remove the core using an apple corer or pastry cutter.

2. Bring 500ml of cold water and the 175g of sugar to the boil in a medium pan. Add the pineapple and simmer for 5 minutes, until just tender. Lift out, drain well, then place on a baking sheet. Rapidly boil the remaining liquid until reduced to 250ml. Set aside.

3. Preheat the grill to High. Brush the steaks with melted butter and grill for 3–4 minutes each side until cooked through and the fat is crisp. Remove, cover and keep warm.

4. Sprinkle each pineapple slice with a good pinch of black pepper and 1 teaspoon of the remaining sugar. Grill for 4–5 minutes, or until nicely caramelised. Remove and drizzle with a little of the pineapple syrup (save the rest for a dessert). Lift the gammon steaks on to warmed plates, top with the caramelised pineapple and serve.

Stuffed beef rolls with tomato and olive sauce

Roll beef steaks around gorgeous stuffing and cook them in a rich tomato sauce to make this easy dish for the whole family.

SERVES 4
READY IN 45 MINUTES

50g butter

2 small onions, 1 finely chopped and 1 finely sliced

½ tsp dried mixed herbs

75g fresh white breadcrumbs

4 x 160–180g thin-cut beef frying steaks

1 tbsp olive oil

1 garlic clove, crushed

400g can chopped tomatoes in natural juice

10 pitted black olives, sliced

Small handful of chopped fresh flatleaf parsley

Mashed or boiled potatoes, to serve

1. Melt the butter in a frying pan over a medium–low heat. Add the chopped onion and cook for 5 minutes, until softened. Add the herbs and cook for 1 minute. Stir in the breadcrumbs and season.

2. Spread each steak with a quarter of the stuffing. Roll up and secure each one in place with a cocktail stick.

3. Heat the oil in a large, deep frying pan over a high heat. Add the beef rolls and brown for a few minutes, turning. Remove and set aside.

4. Add the sliced onion and the garlic to the pan and cook over a medium heat for 5 minutes, until softened and lightly browned. Return the beef to the pan with the tomatoes. Half-fill the empty can with water and add this as well. Scatter with the olives, bring to the boil and simmer for 20 minutes, stirring occasionally, until the beef is cooked through and the sauce has reduced slightly. Season to taste, garnish with the parsley and serve with mashed or boiled potatoes.

Liver and bacon with celeriac mash

The old classic, liver and bacon, is perfect for cold winter evenings and here it is brought into season with celeriac mash.

SERVES 4
READY IN 30 MINUTES

8 rashers dry-cured streaky bacon
350g calf's liver, thinly sliced
Large pinch of caster sugar
1 tbsp plain flour, for dusting
1 tbsp sunflower oil
1 tbsp balsamic vinegar

For the celeriac mash:

2 large (about 450g) potatoes, diced
450g celeriac, diced
3 tbsp skimmed milk
Bunch of spring onions, trimmed and chopped

1. First, make the celeriac mash. Simmer the potatoes and celeriac in a large pan of boiling, salted water for about 15 minutes or until tender. Drain, return to the pan and shake over a low heat for 3–4 minutes to dry out.

2. In a small pan, gently heat the milk. Add the spring onions and cook for 2–3 minutes, until softened. Add to the potatoes and celeriac, then mash and season. Cover and keep hot.

3. Meanwhile, grill the bacon until it begins to crisp at the edges.

4. Season the liver on both sides with salt, pepper and the sugar, then coat lightly in the flour. Heat a large frying pan over a high heat. When hot, add the oil, then the liver and cook for 2 minutes each side, until nicely browned but still pink and juicy on the inside. Add the balsamic vinegar to the pan and shake briefly. Serve the liver and pan juices immediately with the celeriac mash and crispy bacon.

★ DELICIOUS. TIP It's important to cook liver right at the last minute before you serve it, so that it's eaten while tender and juicy.

Ham hock, split pea and mint stew

You can make this dish the night before so that all it requires is heating through the following day. But if you do this, add the mint and blend half the stew just before serving.

SERVES 4
TAKES ABOUT 2 HOURS

600g ham hock
2 carrots, roughly chopped
1 large onion, quartered
6 black peppercorns
150g dried yellow split peas
450g white potatoes, cut
  into cubes
150g frozen peas
Small handful of chopped
  fresh mint, plus extra to serve

1. Put the ham hock, carrots, onion and peppercorns in a large pan. Add 1.7 litres of water, cover and bring to the boil. Reduce the heat and leave to simmer for 1 hour, skimming off any scum as it appears.

2. Strain the cooking liquid through a colander into another large pan. Set the hock aside to cool slightly, pull off the meat and shred. Cover and set aside. Discard the bone and the contents of the colander.

3. Bring the liquid to a simmer. Add the split peas and cook for 35 minutes, skimming off any scum. Add the potatoes and cook for 10–12 minutes or until the potatoes and split peas are tender. Stir in the frozen peas and cook for 2–3 minutes, until soft. Take off the heat and stir in most of the mint. Remove half of the stew to a bowl, blend until smooth, mix with the remaining stew and season.

4. Divide the stew among warmed bowls. Top with the shredded ham and reserved mint to serve.

Quick lamb, orange and fennel spring stew

This satisfying recipe is ideal for a light, one-pot family supper in spring.

SERVES 4
READY IN 45 MINUTES

600g lamb, cubed (see tip
  below)
2 tbsp plain flour, seasoned
2 tbsp olive oil
1 red onion, thinly sliced
2 garlic cloves, chopped
1 tsp fennel seeds
Grated zest and juice of
  2 oranges
300ml fresh chicken stock, hot
500g baby new potatoes
1 large fennel bulb, roughly
  chopped
1 tbsp red wine vinegar
2 tbsp chopped fresh parsley
Steamed spinach or spring
  greens, to serve

1. In a bowl, coat the lamb in the seasoned flour. Heat the oil in a large frying pan over a high heat. Add the lamb, in batches, and brown each batch for 5 minutes. Remove and set aside.

2. Add the onion, garlic and fennel seeds to the pan, and cook for 5 minutes, stirring occasionally, until softened and golden.

3. Stir in the orange zest and juice, the chicken stock, potatoes, fennel and browned lamb. Bring to the boil, then cover and simmer gently for 20 minutes or until the potatoes are tender.

4. Stir in the vinegar and parsley, and adjust the seasoning to taste. Serve in warmed bowls with steamed spinach or spring greens.

★ DELICIOUS. TIP Use ready-cubed lamb or cut up your own choice of cut – for lean meat, choose leg; if you like it slightly fattier, try neck fillet.

Sicilian sausages with roasted sweet potatoes

A simple flavour-packed dinner that needs very little preparation – just pop it all in the tin and roast.

SERVES 2
READY IN 40 MINUTES

6 spicy Sicilian sausages
1 large sweet potato, cubed
6 garlic cloves, unpeeled
2 small preserved or pickled
   lemons, halved
4 fresh rosemary sprigs
1 tbsp olive oil
1 tbsp clear honey
Creamy mash and seasonal
   greens, to serve

1 Preheat the oven to 200ºC/fan 180ºC/gas 6. Place the sausages, sweet potato, garlic cloves, lemons and rosemary sprigs in a roasting tin so that they all sit quite snugly, but in a single layer.

2 In a bowl, mix together the olive oil, honey, 3 tablespoons of water and some salt and pepper. Spoon over the top of the sausage and potato mix. Roast for 30 minutes, turning once or twice, until cooked through and golden.

3 Squeeze the roasted garlic out of their skins to eat – it's deliciously sweet – and serve with creamy mash and seasonal greens.

Variation Spicy Sicilian sausages (with pork and fennel) are now readily available in delis and large supermarkets, but you can use any meaty pork and herb sausages instead. You can also replace the sweet potato with squash, if you wish.

Mexican minced beef and spicy polenta cobbler

A fantastic Mexican-inspired take on an old favourite.

SERVES 8
TAKES 1 HOUR, PLUS 20 MINUTES
IN THE OVEN

4 tbsp sunflower oil
2 medium onions, finely chopped
4 garlic cloves, crushed
1 tsp crushed dried chillies
2 tsp freshly ground cumin
  seeds
1kg lean minced beef
3 tbsp tomato purée
1½ tsp light muscovado sugar
300ml beef stock, hot
200g can chopped tomatoes
2 roasted red peppers from
  a jar, drained and chopped
400g can red kidney beans in
  water, rinsed and drained

For the spicy polenta cobbler:
200g plain flour
1 tbsp baking powder
1 tbsp soft brown sugar
¼ tsp crushed dried chillies
75g polenta
65g Cheddar, finely grated
1 medium egg
175ml milk
2 tbsp sunflower oil
25g butter, melted

1. Heat the oil in a large pan, add the onions and garlic, and cook for 10 minutes, until lightly browned. Add the chillies and cumin, and fry for 2–3 minutes. Add the beef and cook over a high heat, breaking up with a wooden spoon as it browns. Add the purée, sugar, stock and tomatoes and simmer for 25 minutes, until reduced and thickened. Stir in the red peppers and kidney beans. Season and spoon into a 2.75–3-litre shallow ovenproof dish.

2. Preheat the oven to 220°C/fan 200°C/gas 7. Make the cobbler. Sift the flour, baking powder, sugar and ¼ teaspoon of salt into a bowl, and stir in the chillies, polenta and 50g of the grated cheese. Beat the egg, milk, oil and melted butter together, and stir into the dry ingredients.

3. Drop 8 spoonfuls of the mixture around the edge of the dish, about 2.5cm apart, and sprinkle with the remaining grated cheese. Bake for 20 minutes, until bubbling hot and the topping is puffed up and golden.

Steak tagliata with roasted vine tomatoes

For something different, try this quick and easy sirloin steak dish, served with roasted vine tomatoes and rocket.

SERVES 4
READY IN 20 MINUTES

4 strings cherry tomatoes on the vine (each with about 8 tomatoes)

8 tbsp extra-virgin olive oil

4 x 225–250g sirloin steaks

1 tsp Dijon mustard

4 tsp balsamic vinegar

175g rocket

75g Parmesan or Grana Padano, pared into thin shavings

1. Preheat the oven to 180°C/fan 160°C/gas 4. Put the cherry tomatoes, on the vine, into a small roasting tin, drizzle with 3 tablespoons of the olive oil and season. Roast in the oven for 12–15 minutes, until the tomatoes are just tender.

2. Meanwhile, brush the steaks on both sides with 1 tablespoon of the oil, and season. Heat a heavy-based griddle or frying pan over a high heat until smoking. Add the steaks and cook for 2 minutes each side for rare, 3 minutes for medium, a minute or two longer for well done. Lift on to a board to rest.

3. Meanwhile, whisk the mustard and balsamic vinegar together in a small bowl, then whisk in the remaining olive oil. Season to taste and set aside.

4. Spread the rocket over the centre of four plates. Slice each steak slightly on the diagonal and place on top of the salad leaves. Sprinkle over the balsamic dressing, then scatter with the cheese shavings. Serve immediately with the roasted tomatoes.

Indian spiced pork koftas with cumin raita

The word 'kofta' simply means meatball, and these mildly spiced ones are great cooked on the barbecue.

SERVES 4

TAKES 30 MINUTES, PLUS 30 MINUTES SOAKING, AND CHILLING AND RESTING

1 large red onion, finely diced
1 tsp ground cumin
500g minced pork
50g fine breadcrumbs
1 tsp finely chopped red chilli from a jar
1 tsp korma curry powder
3cm piece fresh root ginger, grated
1 tsp ground coriander
2 garlic cloves, crushed
Vegetable oil, for greasing
Warm naan bread, to serve

For the raita:

½ tsp ground cumin
300ml natural yogurt
3 ripe tomatoes, seeded and diced
¼ cucumber, seeded and diced
Squeeze of fresh lemon juice

1. Soak eight wooden skewers in cold water for 30 minutes to prevent them burning during cooking.

2. Meanwhile, put three-quarters of the onion (reserve the rest for the raita) and the cumin into a food processor. Add the rest of the kebab ingredients (except the oil and naan bread), season and whiz together into a ball. Divide into 8 sausage shapes and thread each one on to a skewer. Chill for 20 minutes.

3. Preheat the grill to High. Lay the koftas on a lightly oiled, foil-lined grill pan or baking sheet. Pop under the grill for 15 minutes, turning, until cooked through. Rest for 5 minutes.

4. Meanwhile, make the raita. In a bowl, mix the reserved onion, the cumin, yogurt, tomatoes, cucumber and lemon juice. Season.

5. Put 2 koftas on each plate with a little of the raita and naan bread. Serve with a side salad, if you wish.

Variation You could also make these koftas with minced beef or minced lamb and, if you like things extra spicy, use a madras-style curry powder to add a little extra kick.

Devilled lamb chops

Using tender spring lamb, this dish is Anglo-Indian food at its finest.

SERVES 4

TAKES 45 MINUTES, PLUS A FEW HOURS OR OVERNIGHT MARINATING

1cm cube fresh root ginger

6 garlic cloves

2 tbsp curry powder

1 tsp salt

Juice of 2 limes

4 tbsp live natural yogurt

8 lamb loin or saddle chops, trimmed of excess fat

For the side salad:

1 cucumber, peeled, halved lengthways, seeded and chopped

6 ripe tomatoes, seeded and roughly chopped

2 red onions, finely sliced

Juice of 1 lime

½ tsp salt

½ tsp freshly ground black pepper

3 tbsp mild olive oil or cold-pressed rapeseed oil

Small bunch of fresh mint leaves

Small bunch of fresh coriander leaves

1. Make the marinade. Chop the ginger and garlic to a near paste. Put in a bowl and stir in the curry powder, salt, lime juice and yogurt. Pop the marinade and lamb chops in a plastic bag, and squish around to cover the meat. Chill for a few hours or, ideally, overnight.

2. Just before you cook the lamb chops, preheat the grill to High and put the side salad together. Put the cucumber, tomatoes and onions in a bowl. Combine the lime juice, salt, pepper and oil to make a dressing, and toss with the salad and herbs.

3. Grill the chops for 3–4 minutes each side for medium but a bit pink. Cook for longer, if you prefer your meat less pink. Rest for about 10 minutes before serving; they should be juicier and more tender that way. Serve with the side salad.

★ DELICIOUS. TIP You can also cook these chops on the barbecue over medium–hot coals for 3–4 minutes on each side until charred and golden.

Naan bread pizzas

These make a quick and easy supper that's ideal for eating in front of the telly.

SERVES 2
READY IN 15 MINUTES

4 beef sausages

A good pinch of dried chilli flakes

2 garlic and coriander naan breads

2–4 tbsp crème fraîche

½ red onion, thinly sliced

A small handful of fresh mint leaves, roughly chopped

2 good handfuls of rocket leaves

Olive oil, for drizzling

1. Preheat the grill to Medium. Slit the skins of each sausage and remove the meat. Put a frying pan over a medium heat, add the sausagemeat and dried chilli flakes, and cook for 3–4 minutes, roughly breaking up the sausagemeat with a wooden spoon, until it is well browned and tender.

2. Place the naan breads on a baking sheet and top each one with the browned sausagemeat and a few spoonfuls of crème fraîche. Scatter over the red onion and mint leaves, and grill for 3–4 minutes.

3. Lift the naan on to serving plates and top each one with a handful of rocket leaves. Drizzle over a little olive oil and serve.

chicken and poultry

Rosemary and honey roast chicken with garlic mash

Honey, rosemary and garlic is a classic combination of flavours for this quick and easy dinner.

SERVES 2
TAKES 10 MINUTES, PLUS
20–25 MINUTES IN THE OVEN

2 free-range chicken legs
2 tablespoons runny honey
Juice of 1 small lemon
1 whole garlic bulb
2 small fresh rosemary sprigs
450g pack fresh potato, carrot and swede mash
Steamed French beans, to serve

1. Preheat the oven to 200°C/fan 180°C/gas 6. Slash the chicken legs a few times on the skin side and place in a roasting tin. Drizzle with the honey and the lemon juice, then season well. Cut the whole bulb of garlic in half horizontally and place in the roasting tin with the chicken.

2. Roast for 15 minutes, then baste and tuck the rosemary sprigs under the chicken. Roast for a further 10 minutes or until the chicken is cooked through and golden, and the pan juices sticky.

3. Meanwhile, heat the potato, carrot and swede mash according to the packet instructions. Squeeze the pulp from the roasted garlic cloves and stir into the mash with some seasoning. Serve mounds of mash on warmed serving plates, top with the roast chicken and drizzle over the sticky pan juices. Delicious served with steamed French beans.

Variation For a change, try using maple syrup and thyme instead of the honey and rosemary flavouring.

Chicken and chorizo pilaff

This pilaff is a simplified version of the Spanish paella, and it's just as tasty.

SERVES 4
READY IN 35 MINUTES

2 tbsp olive oil

1 large onion, thinly sliced

2 garlic cloves, crushed

6 boneless skinless chicken
  thighs (about 600g)

Large pinch of saffron

250g long grain rice

200g piece chorizo, thickly
  sliced

600ml chicken stock, hot

Grated zest and juice of
  1 small lemon

Handful of chopped fresh
  flatleaf parsley

1. Heat the oil in a heavy-based saucepan over a medium–high heat. Fry the onion for 4–5 minutes, stirring occasionally, until it starts to turn golden. Add the garlic and cook for a further minute.

2. Add the chicken pieces, chopped into chunks, and cook, stirring occasionally, until golden. Add the saffron and cook for 1 minute. Stir in the rice and chorizo, then pour in the stock. Stir, then bring to a simmer. Season, cover and simmer gently for 20 minutes or until the rice is tender and the stock has been absorbed. Stir in the lemon zest and juice, the parsley, and serve immediately.

Variation Replace the saffron with 2 teaspoons of paprika for a spicier, more authentically paella-style dish. You could also add a few cooked and peeled prawns, if you wish.

Honeyed duck and vegetable stir-fry

Sometimes stir-fries are overloaded with ingredients, but here less means more, and the flavour of the duck shines through.

SERVES 4
READY IN 20 MINUTES

2 tbsp clear honey
4 tbsp dark soy sauce
4 skinless duck breasts
2 carrots
Bunch of spring onions
1 small Chinese leaf head
1 tbsp vegetable oil
Thai fragrant rice, boiled or
    steamed, to serve

1. In a large bowl, mix together the honey and soy sauce. Slice the duck and toss in the honey marinade. Set aside for 5 minutes. Cut the carrots and spring onions into thin strips. Finely shred the Chinese leaf.

2. Heat the oil in a wok or large frying pan. Lift the duck from the marinade (reserve the marinade) and stir-fry for 2 minutes until browned all over. Remove and set aside. Add the carrot and stir-fry for 1 minute. Add the spring onions, Chinese leaf and browned duck. Pour over the marinade and stir-fry for 2–3 minutes – the duck should still be a little pink in the middle (if using chicken, make sure it is cooked through). Season to taste and serve with rice.

★ DELICIOUS. TIP Some supermarkets sell skinless duck breasts. If you can't find any, buy duck breasts with the skin on and simply remove it yourself.

Variation This recipe works equally well with skinless chicken breasts.

Parmesan turkey with roast tomato and basil potatoes

Crunchy, oven-baked goujons of turkey, coated in Parmesan cheese, are roasted alongside some yummy new potatoes.

SERVES 4
TAKES 1 HOUR

800g large new potatoes, unpeeled and quartered

2 tbsp olive oil

250g cherry tomatoes

150g fresh Parmesan, grated

2 large egg whites

4 turkey breast steaks, cut into strips

Small handful of fresh basil leaves, large leaves torn

1 lemon, quartered, to serve

1. Preheat the oven to 220°C/fan 200°C/gas 7. Put the potatoes in a roasting tin, drizzle with the oil, season and mix. Roast for 35 minutes in the oven, turning halfway. Mix in the tomatoes and roast for a further 10 minutes, until they begin to soften.

2. Meanwhile, spread out the Parmesan on a large plate and season with black pepper. Put the egg whites in a bowl and whisk until frothy. Coat the turkey strips in the egg whites, then press each one into the Parmesan roughly to cover. Place them in one layer on a large, lightly greased non-stick baking sheet.

3. When the potatoes have 20 minutes' cooking time left, pop the turkey into the oven. Roast, turning halfway, until cooked through and golden. Drain briefly on kitchen paper.

4. Divide the turkey among four warmed plates. Stir the basil leaves into the potatoes and spoon alongside the turkey. Garnish with the lemon quarters.

Variation If anyone in your family doesn't like turkey, you can try using chicken, or any firm white fish, such as monkfish.

Mediterranean stuffed chicken

This easy chicken recipe offers a real taste of the sun in every mouthful, with goat's cheese, sun-dried tomatoes and fragrant thyme.

SERVES 2
READY IN 30 MINUTES

100g crumbly goat's cheese

240g pack Sun-Blush tomatoes in oil, drained and roughly chopped (reserve 1 tbsp of the oil)

Few fresh thyme sprigs, leaves picked

2 large chicken breasts, skin on

125g dried spaghetti

1. Preheat the oven to 220°C/fan 200°C/gas 7. In a bowl, mix together the cheese, half the Sun-Blush tomatoes and half the thyme. Season with freshly ground black pepper.

2. Cut a slit in the side of the chicken breasts to make a pocket. Stuff each generously with the cheese mixture, put into a small roasting tin and season. Drizzle over the reserved oil, scatter with the rest of the fresh thyme and dot around the remaining Sun-Blush tomatoes. Roast for 20–25 minutes, or until cooked through and golden.

3. Meanwhile, cook the spaghetti according to the packet instructions. Drain and return to the pan. Lift the chicken and any spilt filling on to serving plates. Stir the roasted tomatoes and pan juices into the spaghetti and toss together. Serve with the chicken.

Chicken and spinach curry

You'll be amazed at how good this cheat's curry is – simply made using a tub of spicy mulligatawny soup.

SERVES 4
READY IN 25 MINUTES

125g basmati rice
1 tbsp vegetable oil
4 skinless chicken breasts
600g tub fresh chicken mulligatawny soup
100g fresh baby leaf spinach
Naan bread, to serve (optional)

1. Cook the rice according to the packet instructions, then drain.

2. Meanwhile, heat the oil in a deep frying pan over a high heat. Add the chicken and fry for 2–3 minutes each side to brown all over. Pour in the soup and bring back to the boil. Reduce the heat slightly and partially cover the pan with a lid. Simmer for 15 minutes – turning the chicken halfway – or until the chicken is cooked through and the soup has reduced to form a sauce.

3. Stir the spinach into the sauce, until just wilted. Season. Divide the rice among four warmed bowls and put the chicken on top. Spoon over the sauce and serve with some warmed naan bread, if you wish.

Cheat's coq au vin

The rustic French classic is simplified here for those who want the wonderful flavour but don't have time to cook the traditional version.

SERVES 4
READY IN 30 MINUTES

1 tbsp sunflower oil

4 boneless chicken breasts

150g streaky bacon rashers, chopped

250g chestnut mushrooms, quartered

1 tbsp chopped fresh thyme leaves

3 garlic cloves, 2 chopped and 1 halved

150ml red wine

300g tub fresh chicken gravy

4 baguette slices, cut thickly on the diagonal

Steamed French beans, to serve

1. Heat the oil in a large saucepan. Add the chicken breasts and fry over a medium heat for 5 minutes on each side, or until golden. Remove and set aside.

2. Add the bacon to the pan and fry for 5 minutes, until browned. Stir in the mushrooms, thyme and chopped garlic, and fry for 5 minutes.

3. Return the chicken to the pan, add the wine and bubble until reduced by half. Pour in the chicken gravy and simmer for 5 minutes or until the chicken is cooked through and the sauce has thickened.

4. Toast the baguette slices under the grill and then rub one side with the halved garlic clove. Divide the bread slices among four plates, spoon over the coq au vin and serve with some steamed French beans.

Turkey and apricot burgers with sweet potato wedges

Try a taste of the Mediterranean with these delicious sweet-and-sour turkey and apricot burgers.

SERVES 4
TAKES 20 MINUTES, PLUS 35–40 MIN-
UTES IN THE OVEN; PLUS CHILLING

1 tbsp sunflower oil

1 small onion, finely diced

3 rashers streaky bacon, chopped

1 garlic clove, crushed

2 slices (75g) wholemeal bread, crusts removed

Handful of fresh flatleaf parsley, finely chopped

500g minced turkey

100g dried ready-to-eat apricots, finely chopped

4 burger buns, halved

Little gem lettuce leaves, tomato slices and burger relishes, to serve

For the sweet potato wedges:

900g sweet potatoes, unpeeled

3 tbsp sunflower oil

1. Heat the oil in a frying pan over a medium heat. Add the onion, bacon and garlic, and fry for 5 minutes, until soft and lightly golden. Tip into a bowl and leave to cool.

2. Preheat the oven to 200°C/fan 180°C/gas 6. Meanwhile, whiz the bread and parsley in a food processor to make fine crumbs. Add to the bowl with the turkey and apricots, season, and mix together well. Shape into 4 burgers, then cover and chill for 20 minutes.

3. Cut the sweet potatoes into wedges, put into a large roasting tin with the oil and some seasoning, and toss together. Spread them out, then roast for 35–40 minutes, turning halfway, until tender and golden.

4. About 20 minutes before the wedges are ready, heat a griddle over a medium–high heat. Add the burgers and cook for 7–8 minutes each side until cooked through. Rest for 5 minutes.

5. Toast the burger buns. Divide the lettuce and tomato among each base and top with the burgers and bun tops. Serve with the potato wedges and relishes.

Aromatic Thai duck curry

A wonderfully rich curry for when you feel like something
a little special.

SERVES 4
READY IN 1¼ HOURS

2 x 400ml cans coconut milk
4 duck legs, skinned, then
  halved at the joint
250g small waxy new potatoes
1 tbsp sunflower oil
2 tsp light soft brown sugar
2 tsp fresh lime juice
Handful of fresh coriander
  leaves, to garnish
Steamed rice, to serve

For the curry paste:

1 tsp fennel seeds
1 tbsp coriander seeds
2 tsp cumin seeds
3 pieces blade mace
¼ tsp white peppercorns
2 lemongrass stalks, outer
  leaves discarded
3 medium–hot red chillies,
  seeded (optional) and chopped
65g shallots, chopped
6 large garlic cloves, peeled
25g fresh root ginger, chopped
½ tsp salt
2 tbsp sunflower oil

1. Bring the coconut milk to a simmer in a
medium-sized pan. Add the duck and simmer,
uncovered, for 1 hour, until the meat is tender and
the coconut milk has reduced by half. Lift the duck
on to a plate, cool, then break the meat away from
the bones into large chunks. Reserve the strained
coconut milk.

2. Meanwhile, for the curry paste, toss the seeds
and mace around briefly in a hot frying pan until
aromatic. Grind to a fine powder with the
peppercorns. Put the ground spices into a mini
food processor with the lemongrass, chillies,
shallots, garlic, ginger, salt and oil, and blend to a
smooth paste.

3. Cook the potatoes in a pan of boiling salted
water for 12–15 minutes, until tender. Drain, cool,
then thickly slice.

4. Heat the oil in a pan, add the curry paste and fry
gently for 5 minutes. Add the reserved coconut
milk and simmer until the sauce has thickened.
Stir in the sugar, lime juice, duck and potatoes.
Season and heat through. Garnish with the
coriander leaves, and serve with steamed rice.

Chicken with honey and mustard glaze

Poaching the chicken before glazing it in the oven is a good way of keeping it lusciously moist.

SERVES 4–5
READY IN ABOUT 1½ HOURS

1.75kg chicken joints (cut a
2kg chicken into 10–12 pieces or use 10–12 thighs and/or drumsticks)
2 star anise
2 garlic cloves
1 small onion or shallot, halved
1 carrot, chopped
2 bay leaves
2 tbsp clear honey
2 tbsp wholegrain mustard
2 tbsp olive oil

1. Put the chicken thighs and drumsticks (but not the breasts), into a large saucepan with the star anise, garlic, onion, carrot and bay leaves. Cover with cold water, add 1 teaspoon of salt and bring to the boil. Simmer for 5 minutes, then skim. Cook very gently for a further 30 minutes, adding the breasts after 15 minutes. Cool the chicken in the liquid, then remove and place skin-side up in a foil-lined roasting tin or shallow ovenproof dish (if you want to, strain the stock and keep it as a base for a risotto or soup).

2. Preheat the oven to 200°C/fan 180°C/gas 6. Mix together the honey, mustard and oil, and brush or spoon half of it over the chicken. Season and cook, uncovered, for 10 minutes. Baste with more of the glaze and cook for another 15–20 minutes, until piping hot and nicely glazed.

★ DELICIOUS. TIP This is great eaten hot and sticky from the oven – maybe served with some boiled rice and stir-fried Chinese greens – or eaten cold at a picnic.

Roast chicken with bacon, leek and herb stuffing

A classic roast chicken with a tasty, old-fashioned bacon and herb stuffing.

SERVES 4

TAKES 45 MINUTES, PLUS ABOUT
1¼ HOURS IN THE OVEN

100g rindless smoked streaky
  bacon rashers, cut into strips
75g butter, softened
1 medium onion, chopped
100g leek, washed and sliced
90g crustless day-old white
  bread, cut into 1cm cubes
1 tsp chopped fresh rosemary,
  plus extra sprigs
1 tsp chopped fresh thyme,
  plus extra sprigs
1 tbsp chopped fresh parsley
1 medium egg
4 tbsp milk
1.5kg organic free-range
  chicken
1 tbsp plain flour
About 450ml chicken stock, hot

1. Preheat the oven to 180°C/fan 160°C/gas 4. Fry the bacon in 15g of the butter until golden. Add the onion and cook until lightly golden. Add the leek and cook for 2–3 minutes. Tip into a bowl. Fry the bread cubes in another 25g of butter until crisp and golden. Add to the bowl with the herbs and seasoning, and mix together well. Beat the egg with the milk, stir into the stuffing mixture and leave for 5 minutes.

2. Spoon the stuffing into the chicken's body cavity, push in the extra herbs and seal the opening with a skewer. Truss the chicken, put into a roasting tin and smear with the remaining butter. Season. Roast for 1¼ hours until cooked through.

3. Lift the chicken on to a board and leave to rest. Skim off the excess fat from the pan juices and place over a medium heat. Stir in the flour, then the chicken stock and simmer until slightly thickened. Season. Carve the chicken and serve with the gravy and some vegetables.

Stir-fried chicken and vegetable noodles

Dinner can be on the table in less than half an hour with this scrumptious stir-fry.

SERVES 4–6

READY IN 20 MINUTES

250g dried medium egg noodles

1 tbsp groundnut oil

2 boneless skinless chicken breasts, cut into strips

4 spring onions, trimmed and sliced

Small knob fresh root ginger, finely chopped or grated

200g beansprouts

1 large carrot, cut into matchsticks

125g baby sweetcorn, halved lengthways

150g mangetout, finely sliced lengthways

For the sauce:

2 tbsp soy sauce

2 tbsp oyster sauce

2 tbsp sweet chilli sauce

1. Mix the ingredients for the sauce together and set aside. Cook the noodles according to the packet instructions, drain and set aside.

2. Put a large wok or large, deep frying pan over a high heat. When hot, add the oil and chicken, and stir-fry for 8 minutes, until golden and cooked through. Add the spring onions, ginger, beansprouts, carrot, baby sweetcorn and mangetout. Stir-fry for a further 1 minute.

3. Add the noodles and sauce to the wok, and stir-fry for 1–2 minutes, until well mixed. Serve hot.

Chorizo, wild and red rice-stuffed poussin

Wild rice and red rice are great in salads and stuffings, because of their delicious nutty flavour and texture.

SERVES 4
TAKES 25 MINUTES, PLUS
35 MINUTES IN THE OVEN

100g mixed wild and red rice
100g basmati rice
1 tbsp olive oil, plus extra
  for drizzling
1 small onion, finely chopped
1 celery stick, finely chopped
100g chorizo, roughly chopped
175ml glass white wine
8–10 fresh sage leaves,
  chopped, plus extra whole
  leaves to garnish
2 large poussins
10g butter, softened
Green salad, to serve

1. Preheat the oven to 200°C/fan 180°C/gas 6. Cook the wild rice mix and basmati rice according to the packet instructions. Drain well.

2. Meanwhile, heat the oil in a large frying pan and cook the onion and celery for 10 minutes, until softened. Stir in the chorizo and continue to cook for a few minutes more. Add the wine and simmer over a high heat for about 5 minutes, until nearly all of the wine has evaporated. Remove from the heat and stir in the rice and sage. Season well.

3. Fill the body cavity of each poussin with the rice mixture. Rub the poussins' skin with a little butter, season, and drape a few sage leaves over each breast. Drizzle the sage with a little oil and roast the birds for 35 minutes, until golden and cooked through. Serve with any leftover rice and a green salad.

★ DELICIOUS. TIP Make it even easier by looking out for mixed bags of rice that include all three varieties.

fish and
shellfish

Baked fish with a herb crust and tartare sauce

The crunchy topping helps keep the fish nice and moist. This is lovely served with sautéd potatoes and a crisp green salad.

SERVES 4

TAKES 15 MINUTES, PLUS 10–12 MIN-
UTES IN THE OVEN

Olive oil, for drizzling and
  greasing
4 x 225g thick fish fillets,
  such as hake, haddock or
  sustainably caught cod,
  skinned
75g fresh white breadcrumbs
Finely grated zest of 1 lemon
4 tbsp chopped fresh parsley
1 tbsp snipped fresh chives
1 fat garlic clove, finely chopped
25g butter, melted

For the tartare sauce:
1 egg yolk
1½ tsp white wine vinegar
1½ tsp English mustard
150ml sunflower oil
2 tsp each finely chopped green
  olives, gherkins and capers
2 tsp snipped fresh chives
2 tsp chopped fresh parsley

1. Preheat the oven to 230°C/ fan 210°C/gas 8. Make the tartare sauce. Put the egg yolk, vinegar, mustard and ¼ teaspoon of salt into a food processor and blend briefly. With the machine running, slowly add the oil to make a thick mayonnaise. Transfer to a bowl and stir in the other ingredients.

2. Line a baking sheet with non-stick baking paper and lightly grease it with oil. Season the fish on both sides and lay skinned-side up on the paper.

3. Put the breadcrumbs, lemon zest, parsley, chives, garlic and seasoning into a bowl. Add the butter and stir well with a fork.

4. Divide the crumbs among the fillets and press on top of each piece in a thick, even layer. Drizzle over a little oil and bake for 10–12 minutes or until the crust is crisp and golden and the fish is cooked through. Lift on to warm plates and serve with the tartare sauce.

Salmon, spinach and dill potato bake

Salmon marries well with potato and spinach in this comforting supper dish. It's also perfect as a freezer stand-by.

SERVES 4
TAKES 30 MINUTES

600g waxy potatoes, such as Desirée

About 350g baby leaf spinach

4 skinless salmon fillets, about 700g, cut into bite-sized chunks

1 onion, finely sliced

Finely grated zest of 1 lemon

60g butter

50g flour

500ml semi-skimmed milk

15g fresh dill, chopped

Peas, to serve

1. Cook the unpeeled potatoes in boiling salted water for 15 minutes. Drain and set aside.

2. Meanwhile, put half the spinach in a colander over the sink. Pour over boiling water to wilt the spinach, then refresh in cold water. Repeat. Drain, and squeeze out as much liquid as possible. Set aside in a large bowl, with the salmon, onion and lemon zest.

3. Preheat the oven to 200°C/fan 180°C/gas 6. Make a white sauce. Melt 50g of the butter in a pan over a medium heat. Add the flour and cook, stirring, for 1 minute, then gradually whisk in the milk. Cook for 5 minutes, stirring, until thickened. Season, stir in the dill and cool slightly. Pour over the salmon mixture and gently combine. Tip into a deep, 2.3-litre baking dish.

4. Peel the potatoes and slice thinly. Overlap in a single layer on top of the salmon. Melt the remaining butter and brush over the potatoes. Bake for 50 minutes, or until hot throughout. Serve with peas.

DELICIOUS.TIP You can chill, cover and freeze this dish, unbaked, for up to 2 months, then defrost it at room temperature and bake for 50 minutes.

Variation This would also work well with sea trout, or any firm white fish such as haddock, coley, pollack or sustainably caught cod.

Salad Niçoise

The finest Mediterranean salad that you may ever see, though you won't see it for long once everyone gets a taste.

SERVES 4
READY IN 25 MINUTES

75ml extra-virgin olive oil
Juice of ½ lemon
300g small new potatoes
100g green beans or shelled broad beans
4 free-range eggs, preferably organic
6 ripe tomatoes, cut into eighths
Cos or Little Gem lettuce
225g can tuna in olive oil (not brine)
2 tbsp capers
Generous handful of good olives
8 anchovy fillets in olive oil, drained

1. Mix the oil, lemon juice and some seasoning together to make a dressing.

2. Boil the potatoes until tender, and drain. Unless they are really tiny, break or cut them in half, and toss with about 1 tablespoon of the dressing while still warm. Set aside.

3. Boil the beans until they are tender – about 4 minutes, then refresh under cold water and set aside.

4. Lower the eggs into a pan of boiling water and cook for 6 minutes, by which time the yolks will only be softly set. Drain, cover with cold water, then peel before they are completely cold.

5. To assemble the salad, toss the potatoes, beans, tomatoes, lettuce leaves, tuna, capers and olives in the remaining dressing and either serve in a large bowl or divide among serving plates. Finish the top of the salad with the anchovies and quartered eggs and serve.

Salmon steaks with basil, lemon and olive butter

A simple supper dish with a lot of style.

SERVES 4
READY IN 20 MINUTES

Large handful of fresh basil

1 large lemon

4 pitted black olives, roughly chopped

50g butter, softened

4 salmon steaks, about 175g each

Cooked new potatoes and steamed and sliced baby leeks, to serve

1. Preheat the oven to 200°C/fan 180°C/gas 6. Roughly chop the basil and put into a large bowl. Grate the zest of half the lemon and add to the black olives in another bowl. Add the butter and beat well with a wooden spoon until mixed. Set aside.

2. Season the salmon steaks and put them side by side in a shallow ovenproof dish. Score the zest of the remaining half lemon with a canelle knife, which will remove the zest in strips and give the slices an attractive fluted edge (you don't have to do this, but it looks pretty). Cut 4 slices from the end of the lemon you have just canelled and place one on top of each salmon steak. Divide the olive butter into 4 and spoon on top of each lemon slice. Cover the dish with foil and bake in the oven for 12 minutes or until the fish is just cooked through.

3. Lift the salmon on to warmed plates and spoon over the melted butter. Serve with cooked new potatoes and steamed and sliced baby leeks.

Salmon and cream cheese gnocchi

There's more than one way to use these little Italian potato dumplings, and they are wonderful here in this creamy, slightly spicy oven-bake.

SERVES 4

TAKES 20 MINUTES, PLUS
15–20 MINUTES IN THE OVEN

500g packet fresh gnocchi

25g butter

1 small leek, washed, trimmed and thickly sliced

200g packet soft cheese

2 tbsp tomato purée

½ tsp dried chilli flakes, or to taste

Finely grated zest of 1 lemon

1 tbsp chopped fresh parsley

150g salmon fillet, skinned and diced

1. Preheat the oven to 200°C/fan 180°C/gas 6. Bring a pan of lightly salted water to the boil. Add the gnocchi and cook for 2–3 minutes, until they float to the surface and are cooked. Drain, reserving 250ml of the cooking water. Set aside.

2. Melt the butter in a wide, deep frying pan and gently fry the leek for 3–4 minutes, until soft. Stir in the soft cheese, tomato purée, chilli flakes, lemon zest, parsley and reserved water, and cook gently until the cheese has melted and everything is combined. Adjust the seasoning.

3. Take the pan off the heat and stir in the gnocchi and salmon. Spoon into a deep 1.2-litre ovenproof dish and bake in the oven for 15–20 minutes or until lightly golden on top. Serve immediately.

Variation To make this more economical, you could replace the fresh salmon with canned salmon.

Mussels with chorizo

Seafood with pork is a very Spanish pairing. The sweetness of one plays very well off the saltiness of the other.

SERVES 4
READY IN 25 MINUTES

2kg live mussels

3 tbsp olive oil

1 large onion, finely chopped

200g chorizo, skin removed
  and cut into small chunks
  or rounds

2 garlic cloves, finely chopped

500ml dry white wine

3 tbsp chopped fresh flatleaf
  parsley, plus extra sprigs,
  to garnish

1. Clean the mussels really well, scrubbing the shells and pulling out the beards from between the tightly closed shells. Throw away any that are broken or don't close when tapped on the side of the sink.

2. Heat the olive oil in a large pan, add the onion and sauté for 2–3 minutes, until slightly coloured. Add the chorizo and cook for a further 2 minutes. Add the garlic and cook for 2–3 minutes. Throw in the mussels, pour in the wine and season with black pepper. Cover the pan, bring the liquid to the boil then turn down the heat to Medium for 4–5 minutes, until the mussels steam open.

3. Throw away any mussels that haven't opened. Stir in the chopped parsley and ladle the mussels into soup plates. Garnish with parsley sprigs and serve.

Variation Try using a dry cider here, as they would in parts of northern Spain, instead of the white wine.

Sweet-and-sour chilli prawns

Try a taste of the East with these wonderful sweet-and-sour prawns.

SERVES 4

READY IN 40 MINUTES

Bunch of spring onions, trimmed

3 tbsp sweet chilli sauce

3 tbsp tomato ketchup

1 tbsp caster sugar

1 tbsp light soy sauce

1 tbsp rice wine vinegar or white wine vinegar

3 tbsp sunflower oil

2.5cm piece fresh root ginger, cut into fine matchsticks

500g large raw peeled prawns, deveined if necessary

1 tsp cornflour

2 garlic cloves, crushed

1–2 medium–hot red chillies, seeded and finely chopped

225–275g cherry tomatoes, halved

Noodles or steamed rice, to serve

1. Cut the green tops from the spring onions and cut the tops lengthways into thin shreds. Thinly slice the white parts on the diagonal. Set aside. Mix the chilli sauce, ketchup, sugar, soy sauce and vinegar together in a small bowl.

2. Heat half the oil in a wok or large, deep frying pan. Add the ginger and cook for 30 seconds. Add the prawns and stir-fry for 2 minutes or until just cooked through. Transfer them to a plate.

3. Mix the cornflour with 1 tablespoon of cold water and set aside. Return the wok or pan to the heat and add the remaining oil, garlic and chilli. As soon as they sizzle, add the white spring onions and cherry tomatoes and stir-fry for 30 seconds.

4. Add the chilli sauce mixture and cornflour mixture and simmer for a few seconds until thickened and smooth. Return the prawns to the wok with the shredded green spring onion and toss together well. Serve with noodles or steamed rice.

★ DELICIOUS. TIP To devein a prawn, insert a cocktail stick into their backs about halfway along and hook out the thin black vein with the tip.

Saffron, paprika and garlic seafood stew

A rustic yet sophisticated seafood stew that's a winner with both family and supper guests. Serve with hot garlic bread.

SERVES 4–6

READY IN 35 MINUTES

3 tbsp extra-virgin olive oil

1 large onion, chopped

4 garlic cloves, crushed

2 medium–hot red chillies, halved, seeded and finely chopped

2 tsp sweet paprika

Good pinch of saffron strands

2 strips pared orange zest

4 fresh bay leaves

Leaves from 2 large fresh lemon thyme sprigs

2 x 400g cans chopped tomatoes

300ml dry white wine

50ml well-flavoured chicken or vegetable stock

1 tsp salt

600g cleaned mussels in the shell, fresh or frozen, thawed if frozen

225g cooked peeled tiger prawns, thawed if frozen

400g mixed seafood, such as prawns, mussels, squid, scallops, thawed if frozen

Garlic bread, to serve (optional)

1. Heat the oil in a large casserole or wide shallow saucepan. Add the onion and fry gently for 10 minutes until very soft but not browned. Add the garlic and chillies, and cook for 1 minute. Add the paprika, saffron, orange zest, bay leaves and lemon thyme leaves, and cook for 1 minute more.

2. Add the tomatoes, wine, stock and salt, and bring to the boil. Cover and simmer for 15 minutes.

3. Uncover the stew and stir in the mussels, prawns and mixed seafood. Simmer gently, stirring occasionally, for 5 minutes, until the seafood is heated through – but don't cook it for too long or it will become tough.

4. Ladle the stew into deep bowls and, if you wish, serve with hot garlic bread.

Chunky cod goujons in coconut batter

The coconut in the batter gives this crispy-coated fish a delicious nutty flavour.

SERVES 4
READY IN 20 MINUTES

Sunflower oil, for deep-frying
125g plain flour
1¾ tsp baking powder
2 tbsp Thai fish sauce
50g desiccated coconut
700g thick cod fillet, skinned
25g plain flour, for dusting
2 lemons, halved, to serve
Chunky chips and sweet chilli
  sauce, to serve (optional)

1. Fill a medium heavy-based saucepan two-thirds full with sunflower oil. Heat to 190°C or until a cube of bread added to it browns in 20 seconds. Sift the flour and baking powder into a bowl. Add 175ml of cold water and the Thai fish sauce, and gradually mix together to make a smooth batter. Stir in the coconut and another 1–2 tablespoons of cold water if the batter is a little stiff.

2. Cut the cod into chunky strips, about 2.5cm across. Season with salt, then lightly dust with the flour and shake off the excess. Dip the fish into the batter, then fry in batches (4–5 pieces at a time) for 5 minutes, until crisp and golden brown. Lift out and drain briefly on kitchen paper.

3. Divide the cod goujons among four serving plates. Serve with the lemon halves to squeeze over and some oven-baked chunky chips and sweet chilli sauce, if you like.

Fish curry

Unlike many meat curries, this one is quick to prepare and quick to cook, but it's just as delicious.

SERVES 4
READY IN 30 MINUTES

1 tbsp mild olive oil
400ml can coconut milk
200ml chicken or fish stock, hot
250g potatoes, diced into
2cm cubes
150g fine green beans, trimmed
450g skinless white fish, such as haddock, hake or pollack, cut into bite-sized chunks
Juice of ½ lime, to taste (optional)
Chopped fresh coriander, lime wedges and steamed jasmine rice, to serve

For the curry paste:

1 onion, roughly chopped
2 garlic cloves
2.5cm piece fresh root ginger
3 medium–hot red chillies, seeded (optional)
1 tsp ground coriander
1 tbsp tamarind paste
1 tsp ground turmeric
2 tsp curry powder
1 lemongrass stalk, outer layer discarded and finely chopped
Dash of olive oil, to loosen (optional)

1. Put all the curry paste ingredients in a food processor with a pinch of salt and whiz until smooth. Add a dash of oil to get it moving if it's a little dry.

2. Heat the oil in a wide frying pan over a medium–low heat. Add the paste and cook, stirring occasionally, for 5 minutes, until fragrant – be careful not to burn it.

3. Gently stir the coconut milk into the curry paste, then add the stock and bring to the boil. Add the potatoes, then reduce the heat slightly and simmer for about 10 minutes, until just cooked.

4. Add the beans and cook for 3 minutes, then add the fish and cook for a further 3 minutes, until just cooked through. Remove from the heat and season to taste. You may want to add a dash of lime juice at this stage. Garnish with coriander and lime wedges, and serve with jasmine rice.

Fish pie

A touch of Parmesan cheese and cream in the sauce makes
this version of the classic fish dish extra special.

SERVES 4 (GENEROUSLY)
TAKES ABOUT 40 MINUTES,
PLUS 30 MINUTES IN THE OVEN

1.25kg potatoes, cut into
  even-sized pieces

50g butter

Small bag of fresh baby leaf
  spinach, washed and
  drained

2 shallots, very finely chopped

2 bay leaves

Splash of extra-virgin olive oil

284ml carton double cream

125g Parmesan, grated

Juice of ½ lemon

A handful of flatleaf parsley,
  roughly chopped

450g cod or haddock fillet,
  skinned and cut into bite-sized
  pieces

250g large shelled tiger
  prawns

1. Preheat the oven to 200°C/fan 180°C/gas 6.
Cook the potatoes in boiling, salted water for
10–12 minutes until tender. Drain well, return to
the pan and mash with half the butter and plenty
of seasoning. Set aside.

2. Meanwhile, cook the spinach in a clean pan until
the leaves are just wilted. Drain well, squeeze out
any excess moisture then break up with a knife.

3. In a separate pan, gently cook the shallots and
bay leaves in the oil for 6–8 minutes until softened.
Add the cream and bring just to the boil. Remove
from the heat. Stir in the Parmesan, lemon juice,
and parsley.

4. Toss the fish, prawns and spinach together, and
spread out over the base of a buttered 1.8-litre
shallow ovenproof dish. Remove the bay leaves
from the sauce and pour it evenly into the dish.
Spoon over the mash and dot with the remaining
butter. Put on a baking sheet and bake for
25–30 minutes, until golden and bubbling.

Variation You can use any firm white fish,
unsmoked or smoked, for this pie. A handful
of shelled mussels also goes down very nicely.

Tuna with tomato and caper salsa and pesto beans

This Italian tuna recipe is full of the flavours of the Med, with the added bonus of caper salsa and green pesto beans.

SERVES 4
READY IN 20 MINUTES

4 x 200g tuna steaks, cut about 3cm thick
Olive oil, for brushing

For the salsa:

2 large vine-ripened tomatoes, skinned and roughly chopped
1 large shallot, halved and thinly sliced into fine wedges
1 garlic clove, thinly sliced
1 green chilli, seeded and finely chopped
Pinch of crushed dried chillies
1 tbsp small capers, drained and rinsed
Juice of 1 lime
1 tbsp olive oil
1 tbsp each chopped fresh mint and flatleaf parsley

For the pesto green beans:

40g fresh basil leaves
25g pine nuts
1 garlic clove, crushed
5 tbsp olive oil
25g finely grated Parmesan
500g fine green beans

1. Make the salsa. Mix the tomatoes, shallot, garlic, chillies, capers, lime and oil together in a bowl, and set aside.

2. Make the pesto beans. Bring a pan of salted water to the boil. Meanwhile, whiz the basil, pine nuts, garlic and oil to a paste in a mini food processor. Stir in the Parmesan. Cook the beans in the boiling water for 4–5 minutes, or until tender. Drain, return to the pan with half the pesto and mix well.

3. Brush the tuna with oil, then season. Heat a cast-iron griddle over a high heat. Add the tuna, reduce the heat, and cook for 1½ minutes on each side, until nicely marked on the outside but still quite rare in the centre.

4. Transfer the tuna to 4 plates. Add the mint, parsley and a little salt to the salsa. Serve with the tuna steaks and pesto green beans.

★ DELICIOUS. TIP The leftover pesto will keep, covered, in the fridge for up to 2 days. Or you can freeze it in an ice-cube tray for later use.

Smoked haddock fishcakes with horseradish mayo

Don't be put off by horseradish in the mayo – it adds a slight pepperiness, which complements the fishcakes beautifully.

SERVES 4
TAKES 50 MINUTES, PLUS CHILLING

600g potatoes, roughly chopped

400g undyed smoked haddock fillet

3 tbsp olive oil

1 tbsp capers, drained and chopped

Grated zest of 1 lemon

Small handful of chopped fresh parsley

1 medium egg yolk

Plain flour, for dusting

Lemon wedges and dressed mixed salad, to serve

For the horseradish mayo:

150g good-quality mayonnaise

1–2 tbsp creamed hot horseradish, to taste

Fresh lemon juice, to taste

1. Cook the potatoes in boiling, salted water for 15–20 minutes or until tender. Drain well, return to the pan, mash and set aside, covered.

2. Meanwhile, preheat the grill to Medium–High. Put the haddock in a roasting tin and brush with 1 tablespoon of oil. Grill for 8–10 minutes or until just cooked through. Set aside to cool, then flake into chunks, discarding the skin and any bones.

3. Gently fold the haddock, capers, lemon zest, parsley and egg yolk into the mash, and season. Shape the mixture into 8 fishcakes, cover and chill for 20 minutes or overnight.

4. Meanwhile, mix together the mayonnaise, horseradish, lemon juice and some salt and pepper in a bowl. Cover and chill until needed.

5. Heat the remaining olive oil in a frying pan over a medium heat. Dust the fishcakes with a little flour and fry for 3–4 minutes each side, until golden. Serve with the horseradish mayo, lemon wedges and a dressed mixed salad.

Deep-fried lemon sole with green mayonnaise

Once in a while, some crunchy deep-fried fish fillets just hit the spot. Serve them with salad instead of chips for a change.

SERVES 4
READY IN 25 MINUTES

Sunflower oil, for deep-frying
50g plain flour
2 large eggs, beaten
100g fresh ciabatta
  breadcrumbs
¼ tsp cayenne pepper
12 x 65g skinned lemon sole
  fillets
Lemon wedges, to serve

For the green mayonnaise:

15g mixed fresh flatleaf
  parsley, tarragon and basil
  leaves
15g watercress leaves
15g baby spinach leaves
6 tbsp good-quality
  mayonnaise
2 tsp fresh lemon juice

1. Make the green mayonnaise. Drop the herbs, watercress and spinach into boiling water, cook for 1 minute, then drain and refresh under cold water. Squeeze out the excess water, put into a mini food processor and whiz to a smooth paste. Mix with the mayonnaise and lemon juice, then season and chill until needed.

2. Heat some oil for deep-frying to 190°C. (The oil is ready when a cube of bread added to it browns in 20 seconds.)

3. Season the flour and put on to a plate. Pour the eggs into a shallow dish. Mix the breadcrumbs with the cayenne and a pinch of salt in another shallow dish.

4. Season the fish fillets lightly, then dip, one at a time, in the flour, beaten egg and then the breadcrumbs to coat. Deep-fry, two pieces at a time, for 2 minutes, until crisp and golden. Drain on kitchen paper and keep warm while you cook the remainder. Serve hot with the green mayonnaise and lemon wedges.

meat-free suppers

Green Thai curry with greens

Give your greens some gusto with this vegetarian Thai curry
sauce mixed with broad beans, courgettes and asparagus.

SERVES 4
READY IN 35 MINUTES

Vegetable oil

400ml can coconut milk

3 courgettes, thickly sliced

250g fresh broad beans,
  skins removed

250g asparagus, halved

10 fresh basil leaves

Jasmine rice and lime wedges,
  to serve

For the Thai curry paste:

1 tsp each cumin and coriander
  seeds

5 green Thai bird's eye chillies,
  seeded (optional)

2 shallots, roughly chopped

2 garlic cloves, roughly
  chopped

4cm piece fresh root ginger,
  grated

2 lemongrass stalks, roughly
  chopped

6 kaffir lime leaves or finely
  grated zest of 1 lime

¼ tsp ground turmeric

½ tbsp palm sugar

Handful of fresh coriander
  leaves, plus extra to serve

Splash of vegetable oil

1. Make the curry paste. Heat a dry, heavy-based
frying pan over a medium–high heat. Add the
spices and shake them around for a few seconds
until they smell aromatic. Grind to a fine powder.
Transfer to a mini food processor, add the
remaining paste ingredients and some black
pepper, and whiz for 5 minutes, until smooth.
Set aside.

2. Warm some oil in a large pan over a low heat.
Add 40g of the curry paste and cook for 2 minutes,
stirring. Add the coconut milk, bring to the boil,
then simmer for 5 minutes.

3. Toss the courgettes in a little oil, season, and fry
on a hot griddle for 2 minutes each side. Add to the
curry and cook for 6 minutes. Add the asparagus
and broad beans, and cook for 3–4 minutes, then
stir in the basil. Serve with jasmine rice and lime
wedges to squeeze over.

★ DELICIOUS. TIP The leftover curry paste will keep
in the freezer for up to 3 months.

Tomato, red onion and crème fraîche tart

This wonderful tart is ideal as a supper for friends, and any leftovers will make a great portable lunch or snack.

SERVES 4

TAKES 45 MINUTES, PLUS ABOUT
1 HOUR IN THE OVEN, AND CHILLING
AND COOLING

300g chilled shortcrust pastry
2 tbsp olive oil, plus extra to
  drizzle
3 large red onions, finely sliced
2 garlic cloves, crushed
2 tbsp light muscovado sugar
2 fresh rosemary sprigs,
  leaves picked and chopped
200ml tub crème fraîche
1 medium egg yolk
500g baby plum tomatoes
Mixed salad and crusty bread,
  to serve

1. Preheat the oven to 200°C/fan 180°C/gas 6. Roll out the pastry and use to line a 23cm x 4cm deep loose-bottomed tart tin. Prick the base with a fork and chill for 20 minutes.

2. Line the pastry case with baking paper and beans. Bake for 10 minutes, remove the paper and beans, and bake for a further 10–15 minutes, until golden.

3. Meanwhile, make the tart filling. Heat the oil in a pan, add the onions, cover and cook gently for 10 minutes. Uncover, stir in the garlic, sugar and rosemary, then increase the heat and cook for 8–10 minutes, until golden. Season, cool, then spoon into the pastry case.

4. Mix the crème fraîche, egg yolk and some seasoning, and pour over the onions. Halve 125g of the tomatoesand arrange them in the pastry case together with the whole ones, then drizzle with oil and bake for 25–30 minutes, until golden and softly set.

5. Cool in the tin for 30 minutes. Remove, cut into wedges and serve with a mixed salad and crusty bread.

Vegetable stew with herb dumplings

Full of nutritious vegetables and flavour, this healthy stew is even better with some fluffy, tasty dumplings.

SERVES 4
READY IN ABOUT 1 HOUR

25g butter

1 onion, chopped

1 leek, thickly sliced and washed

3 carrots, roughly chopped

2 celery sticks, roughly chopped

3 tbsp plain flour

600ml vegetable stock or water, hot

410g can mixed pulses, drained and rinsed

Few fresh thyme sprigs

Seasonal greens, to serve

For the herb dumplings:

225g self-raising flour

110g vegetable suet

2 tbsp fresh thyme leaves

1. Melt the butter in a large saucepan over a medium heat. Add the onion and fry for 5 minutes, until softened. Add the leek, carrots and celery, and continue cooking for a further 10 minutes, stirring occasionally, until softened.

2. Stir in the flour, then gradually stir in the stock or water. Add the drained pulses and thyme, cover, and simmer for 20 minutes.

3. Meanwhile, make the dumplings. Mix together the flour, suet and thyme in a bowl, and season. Add about 125ml of cold water to form a soft, slightly sticky dough – add a touch more water if it seems a little dry.

4. Uncover the pan and drop 12 large spoonfuls of the dough into the simmering stew, pushing them in so they're just poking out. Cover again and simmer for a further 20 minutes, until the dumplings are risen and no longer sticky. Serve with seasonal greens.

Variation For a non-veggie version of this stew, cut 2 skinless chicken breasts into pieces and pan-fry for 2 minutes before adding the onion, and use only 2 carrots.

Aubergine and chestnut tagine with herb couscous

Who needs meat when vegetables can taste this good?

SERVES 6
READY IN 1¼ HOURS

1 tbsp ground coriander
2 tsp ground turmeric
1 tbsp ground cinnamon
3 tbsp olive oil
1 red onion, finely chopped
1 red chilli, finely chopped
2 garlic cloves, crushed
50g dates, finely chopped
2cm piece fresh root ginger, grated
500g (2 small) aubergines, cut into 2cm cubes
600g pumpkin or squash, seeded peeled and cut into 3cm cubes
200g cooked peeled chestnuts
2 x 400g cans plum tomatoes
Handful each of fresh mint and coriander, chopped, plus extra coriander to garnish
Juice of 2 lemons

For the herb couscous:

450g couscous
2 tbsp olive oil
5 shallots, sliced
Handful each of finely chopped fresh coriander and parsley

1. Heat a large saucepan over a medium heat. Add the coriander, turmeric and cinnamon, and dry-fry for 1 minute. Add the oil, onion, chilli, garlic, dates and ginger, and cook, stirring occasionally, for 5 minutes, until the onion is softened.

2. Add the aubergines, cook for 5 minutes, then stir in the pumpkin, chestnuts, tomatoes and 100ml of water. Break the tomatoes up into chunks with a spoon and simmer, stirring occasionally, for 25 minutes.

3. Meanwhile, put the couscous into a bowl and season. Pour over 450ml of boiling water, add half the oil and stir once. Cover and set aside for 5–10 minutes, until tender. Fluff up the couscous with a fork.

4. Heat the remaining oil in a frying pan over a medium heat. Add the shallots and fry, stirring occasionally, for 6–8 minutes or until soft and golden. Stir into the couscous with the fresh herbs. Season to taste.

5. Stir the mint, coriander and lemon juice into the tagine. Serve with the couscous.

Stilton and leek bread and butter bake

A tasty, cheesy, main-course version of the classic British pudding.

SERVES 4
TAKES 15 MINUTES, PLUS
30–40 MINUTES IN THE OVEN
AND 20 MINUTES SOAKING

30g butter

2 large leeks, trimmed, cut into medium-sized slices and washed

1 tbsp Dijon mustard

8 medium slices Granary bread

3 eggs

500ml full cream milk

200g Stilton, crumbled

200g Cheddar, grated

Steamed seasonal vegetables, to serve

1. Heat 10g of the butter in a large frying pan over a medium–low heat. Add the leeks and fry gently for 6–8 minutes, stirring occasionally, until softened but not coloured. Set aside.

2. Meanwhile, thinly spread the remaining butter and the mustard on one side of each slice of bread. Cut each slice into quarters. In a large jug, beat the eggs, milk and some seasoning.

3. Preheat the oven to 190°C/ fan 170°C/gas 5. Arrange a third of the bread, buttered-side up, in a shallow ovenproof dish. Scatter with a third of the leeks and a third of the cheeses, then pour over a third of the milk mixture, evenly and slowly. Repeat to use up the remaining ingredients, then leave to soak for 20 minutes or so, if you have time.

4. Place the dish on a baking sheet and cook for 30–40 minutes, until risen and golden. Serve warm with steamed seasonal vegetables.

Variation For a meaty version of this dish, fry 6 crumbled, skinned pork sausages until golden, then add to the leeks before layering up.

Cauliflower and macaroni cheese

This macaroni cheese recipe with a twist is an inspirational vegetarian dish even the most ardent meat lover will love.

SERVES 4

TAKES 20 MINUTES, PLUS
20–25 MINUTES IN THE OVEN

200g dried macaroni

300g cauliflower, broken into florets

50g butter

50g plain flour

600ml milk

50g mature vegetarian Cheddar or Lancashire cheese, grated

1 tbsp Dijon mustard

25g vegetarian Parmesan, grated

Bunch of spring onions, finely sliced

6 large ripe tomatoes, thickly sliced

75g fresh breadcrumbs

Leaves from 2 fresh thyme sprigs, plus extra sprigs, to garnish

2 tbsp extra-virgin olive oil, to drizzle

1. Preheat the oven to 200°C/fan 180°C/ gas 6. Cook the macaroni in boiling salted water for 3 minutes, then add the cauliflower and cook for a further 3 minutes. Drain and return to the pan.

2. Melt the butter in a medium pan. Stir in the flour, remove from the heat and gradually whisk in the milk until smooth. Return to the heat and bring to a simmer, stirring, until thick enough to coat the back of a wooden spoon – about 5 minutes.

3. Stir the Cheddar or Lancashire cheese, mustard and half of the Parmesan into the sauce and season well. Pour the sauce over the macaroni and cauliflower, and fold in the onions. Spoon into a 2-litre ovenproof dish and arrange the tomatoes over the top.

4. Mix the breadcrumbs with the thyme and remaining Parmesan. Sprinkle over the top and drizzle with the oil. Bake for 20–25 minutes, until the top is golden and crusty and the filling is bubbling. Leave to stand for 5 minutes before serving.

Baked stuffed tomatoes

You know that eating a healthy diet containing fruit, vegetables and wholegrains is good for you – but that doesn't mean you should sacrifice flavour!

SERVES 4
READY IN JUST OVER 1 HOUR

1 red pepper
150g brown basmati rice
4 large beef tomatoes
2 tbsp olive oil
1 medium onion, chopped
2 garlic cloves, crushed
Leaves from 3 fresh
  thyme sprigs
4 spring onions, trimmed and
  chopped
Grated zest of 1 lemon
1 tbsp each chopped fresh
  oregano, basil and parsley
50g toasted flaked almonds,
  crumbled
25g finely grated Parmesan
Spinach, to serve

1. Preheat the oven to 220°C/fan 200°C/gas 7. Roast the red pepper for 25 minutes, then seal in a plastic bag and cool. Remove the stalk, seeds and skin, and chop the flesh.

2. Meanwhile, bring a pan of salted water to the boil, add the rice and cook for 25 minutes. Drain. Lower the oven temperature to 190°C/fan 170°C/gas 5.

3. Remove a 1cm slice off the rounded top of each tomato and finely chop. Scoop out and discard the flesh from the tomatoes, upturn them on to kitchen paper and drain.

4. Heat the oil in a pan, add the onion, garlic and thyme, and cook for 10 minutes, until lightly browned. Add the chopped tomato and spring onions, and cook for 1 minute. Remove from the heat and stir in the rice, red pepper, lemon zest, herbs, almonds, 15g of the Parmesan and some seasoning.

5. Spoon the rice mixture into the scooped out tomatoes. Put into an oiled ovenproof dish. Sprinkle with the remaining Parmesan and bake for 30 minutes. Serve with spinach.

Roasted squash and red pepper salad with sun-dried tomato dressing

This beautiful summer salad is packed with wonderful things.

SERVES 4
READY IN 30–40 MINUTES

1 red and 1 yellow pepper
800g butternut squash
2 tbsp olive oil
2 garlic cloves, chopped
½ tsp crushed dried chillies
130g bag mixed watercress,
 spinach and rocket salad
 leaves
Handful of mixed fresh
 coriander and mint leaves
400g can chickpeas, drained
 and rinsed

For the sun-dried tomato
dressing:

6 sun-dried tomatoes in olive
 oil, drained and roughly
 chopped
3 tbsp red wine vinegar
1 garlic clove
1 tbsp balsamic vinegar
7 tbsp extra-virgin olive oil
½ tsp caster sugar
Pinch of crushed dried chillies

1. Preheat the oven to 200°C/fan 180°C/gas 6. Meanwhile, make the dressing. Put the sun-dried tomatoes and vinegar in a small pan, and heat gently for a few minutes until warmed through. Set aside for 30 minutes. Put into a mini food processor with the rest of the ingredients and blend until chunky. Stir in 1 tablespoon of warm water and season.

2. Cook the peppers in a roasting tin for 30 minutes, then seal in a plastic bag and leave to cool. Remove the stalks, skin and seeds, and thinly slice the flesh.

3. Meanwhile, quarter, seed and peel the squash. Cut into 1cm pieces. Toss in a roasting tin with the oil, garlic and chilli, and season. Roast for 20 minutes, until tender.

4. Divide the salad leaves and herbs among four plates. Scatter with the peppers, squash and two-thirds of the chickpeas. Stir the rest of the chickpeas into the dressing. Spoon over the dressing and serve.

Vegetable curry

This is an unusual dish, with its mix of curry powder and coconut milk, but it is an extremely light, easy and tasty curry to prepare.

SERVES 4
READY IN 40 MINUTES

4 garlic cloves, chopped

1.5cm piece fresh root ginger, chopped

1 tsp ground white or black pepper

2 tbsp vegetable oil

2 tbsp curry powder

450g (about 2 medium) waxy potatoes, roughly chopped into about 8 pieces

2 x 400g cans coconut milk

400g can chickpeas, drained and rinsed

1 small cauliflower, cut into small florets

3 tomatoes, each cut into 8 wedges

2 bunches of spring onions, trimmed and halved

2 tbsp soy sauce

1 tsp salt

½ tsp caster sugar

Large handful of fresh coriander leaves, to garnish

Steamed rice or naan bread, to serve

1. Put the garlic, ginger and pepper into a mini food processor, and whiz into a rough paste. Heat the oil in a wok, add the paste and fry for a few minutes over a medium heat. Stir in the curry powder, potatoes, coconut milk and chickpeas, and simmer for 8–10 minutes.

2. When the potato is tender, add the cauliflower. Cook for 5 more minutes, then add the tomato wedges, spring onions, soy sauce, salt and sugar. Cook for another 5 minutes or so. Garnish generously with the coriander leaves and serve with plenty of steamed rice or crispy naan bread.

Spinach and mushroom crêpe bake

This speedy suppertime dish is made even quicker by using ready-made crêpes from the supermarket.

SERVES 4

TAKES 25 MINUTES, PLUS
25 MINUTES IN THE OVEN

500g chestnut mushrooms, sliced

1 tbsp olive oil

2 garlic cloves, crushed

500g baby spinach leaves

8 ready-made savoury pancakes (from supermarket chiller cabinets)

Tomato salad, to serve

For the sauce:

50g butter

50g plain flour

600ml milk

Large pinch of freshly grated nutmeg

100g Gruyère, grated

1. Preheat the oven to 190°C/fan 170°C/gas 5. Fry the mushrooms in the oil over a medium heat for 4–5 minutes until golden. Add the garlic, cook for 1 minute, then season. Tip into a sieve over a bowl to drain. Discard the liquid.

2. Pack the spinach into a large pan and wilt over a high heat. Tip into a colander and press to remove the excess liquid.

3. For the sauce, over a low heat, melt the butter in a pan and stir in the flour. Cook for 2 minutes then, off the heat, slowly whisk in the milk, until smooth. Return to the heat and simmer for 2 minutes until thickened. Season, then stir in the nutmeg and a third of the cheese.

4. Lay the pancakes on a board and top with some spinach, mushrooms and a little sauce. Roll up and place side by side in a large baking dish. Pour over the remaining sauce, scatter with the remaining cheese and bake for 25 minutes. Serve with a tomato salad.

Variation This dish would also work really well with a handful of prawns or some diced salmon.

Aubergine, tomato and mozzarella gratin

Packed full of Mediterranean flavours, this makes the perfect summertime supper dish.

SERVES 8
TAKES 30 MINUTES, PLUS
25–30 MINUTES IN THE OVEN
AND DRAINING

1.2kg aubergines, trimmed
3 x 125g tubs buffalo
  mozzarella, drained and
  sliced
150ml extra-virgin olive oil
2 garlic cloves, crushed
2 x 400g cans cherry tomatoes
  or chopped tomatoes
75g pitted green olives, sliced
12 fresh basil leaves, torn into
  small pieces, plus extra small
  whole leaves to garnish
75g Parmesan, finely grated

1. Cut each aubergine lengthways into thin slices. Lightly sprinkle with salt and leave to drain in a colander for 40 minutes. Pat dry with kitchen paper. Lay the mozzarella slices on kitchen paper.

2. Meanwhile, put 4 tablespoons of the olive oil and the garlic into a large, deep frying pan over a medium–high heat. Add the tomatoes and simmer for 4–5 minutes until thickened slightly. Season.

3. Preheat the oven to 190°C/fan 170°C/gas 5. Heat a large, dry frying pan over a medium–high heat. Brush a few aubergine slices with oil and fry for 3–4 minutes on each side, until golden. Set aside while you cook the remainder.

4. Overlap half the aubergine slices over the base of a deep 2.5-/2.75-litre ovenproof dish. Spoon over half the sauce, scatter over half the olives and half the basil, cover with half the mozzarella slices, then half the grated cheese. Repeat the layers once more. Bake for 25–30 minutes, until golden and bubbling. Serve immediately, garnished with extra whole basil leaves.

Taleggio and mushroom pastry melt

Crisp, rich and delicious, all this needs is a dressed leafy salad to go with it.

SERVES 4

TAKES 15 MINUTES, PLUS 15 MINUTES
IN THE OVEN, PLUS CHILLING

25g butter
1 tbsp olive oil
250g mushrooms, thinly sliced
1 garlic clove, crushed
1 tbsp fresh thyme leaves,
  plus extra to garnish
375g fresh puff pastry
50g rocket leaves
300g taleggio cheese, thinly
  sliced
1 egg, beaten
Dressed leafy salad, to serve

1. Heat the butter and olive oil in a frying pan over a high heat. Add the sliced mushrooms and cook until softened. Reduce the heat, add the garlic and thyme leaves, season with pepper, and cook for 2 minutes. Leave to cool.

2. Roll out the pastry on a lightly floured surface into a 40cm square. Scatter the rocket over one half of the pastry, then top with the mushrooms and sliced taleggio. Brush the pastry edges with beaten egg and fold the other half of the pastry over the filling, pressing the edges together to seal.

3. Carefully lift on to a greased baking sheet and prick here and there with a fork. Chill for 30 minutes. Meanwhile, preheat the oven to 220°C/fan 200°C/gas 7.

4. Brush the pastry with beaten egg and make a few slashes in the top. Bake for 15 minutes, until crisp and golden. Cut into squares, garnish with the fresh thyme leaves and serve hot with a dressed leafy salad.

Vegetable biryani

For a more substantial supper, serve this aromatic rice dish
topped with some quartered hard-boiled eggs.

SERVES 4
READY IN 50 MINUTES

275g basmati rice
40g ghee or butter
1 large onion, finely sliced
2 garlic cloves, crushed
Thumb-sized piece of fresh
  ginger, grated
½ tsp ground turmeric
1 tsp mild chilli powder
1 tsp ground coriander
500g mixed vegetables,
  prepared and cut into small
  pieces (we used cauliflower,
  red pepper, green beans
  and mushrooms)
6 cardamom pods, cracked
6 cloves
Small handful of fresh
  coriander, to garnish
Mango chutney, yogurt and
  poppadoms, to serve

1. Rinse the rice, then leave to soak in cold water
for 30 minutes.

2. Meanwhile, heat the ghee or butter in a large
flameproof casserole dish with a tight-fitting lid
over a medium-high heat. Add the onion and cook
for 10 minutes. Add the garlic, ginger and ground
spices and cook for 2 minutes. Stir in the
vegetables and 150ml of water, cover and cook for
3–4 minutes. Season with plenty of freshly ground
black pepper, then set aside.

3. Preheat the oven to 150°C/fan 130°C/gas 2. Drain
the rice and cook in a pan of boiling salted water
with the whole spices for 5 minutes. Drain well.
Lightly fold into the vegetable mixture.

4. Place the casserole back over a high heat, cover
and cook for 1 minute to build up steam. Transfer
to the oven and cook for 15 minutes, until the rice
and vegetables are tender. Spoon into bowls,
garnish with fresh coriander and serve with mango
chutney, yogurt and poppadoms.

cheese and eggs

Spicy salami, roasted pepper and taleggio frittata

Roasted peppers, in jars, are an excellent time-saving ingredient.
Use any soft Brie-style cheese if you can't find taleggio.

SERVES 4
READY IN 40 MINUTES

400g new potatoes
6 large free-range eggs
200g jar roasted red peppers, drained and sliced into strips
100g thinly sliced spicy salami
150g taleggio or any soft Brie-style cheese, rind removed and cubed
Large handful of fresh basil leaves
2 tbsp olive oil
50g wild rocket
Juice of ½ lemon

1. Boil the potatoes for 7–10 minutes, until tender. Drain, cool, and peel away the skins. Cut into 5mm-thick slices.

2. Crack the eggs into a bowl and beat, then add the potatoes and most of the red peppers. Tear the salami into large pieces and stir most into the egg mixture with the cheese, most of the basil and some seasoning.

3. Preheat the grill to Medium. Heat half the oil in a 23cm, non-stick, ovenproof frying pan over a low heat and carefully tip in the egg mixture. Arrange the remaining pepper strips and salami on top, and cook very gently for 8–10 minutes, until nearly set.

4. Place the frying pan under the grill for a further 2–3 minutes, until set and golden. Cool for a few minutes, then slide the frittata out on to a chopping board. Place the rocket and remaining basil in a bowl, and toss with the remaining olive oil and lemon juice. Cut the frittata into wedges and serve, topped with the basil and rocket.

Variation You can pop almost anything into a frittata. Replace the red peppers with canned artichoke hearts, blanched broad beans, peas or cooked butternut squash. If you don't fancy salami, replace with crispy bacon or Parma ham, and use any cheese that you prefer.

A very Anglo-Indian egg curry

This is good with rice, but you can't beat it with wilted spinach and lemon wedges – served cold, it is a great picnic salad.

SERVES 3–4
READY IN 40 MINUTES

6 medium eggs
400g potatoes, cut into medium dice
1 tsp coriander seeds
1 tsp cumin seeds
Seeds of 3 cardamom pods
½ tsp ground ginger
½ tsp ground turmeric
¼ tsp crushed dried chilli (optional), plus extra to garnish
15g butter
1 tbsp olive oil
3 garlic cloves, chopped
2 medium onions, finely diced
3 celery sticks, finely diced
2 tbsp passata
284ml carton double cream
Coriander leaves, to garnish

1 Cook the eggs in boiling water for 8 minutes. Drain, cool slightly and shell. Set aside.

2 Meanwhile, cook the potatoes in boiling salted water for about 6 minutes, until tender but not falling apart. Drain and set aside.

3 Grind the coriander, cumin and cardamom seeds in a pestle and mortar, then mix with the rest of the spices. Put a large, deep frying pan over a medium heat. When hot, add the spices and dry-fry for 1 minute, until fragrant. Add the butter and oil and, when it fizzes, add the garlic, onions and celery. Fry for 10–12 minutes, until they start to brown.

4 Add the potatoes, passata and cream to the pan and gently warm through. Season to taste. Quarter the eggs. Divide the curry among three or four plates, then place the eggs on top or stir through, if you prefer. Garnish with coriander leaves and, if you wish, some extra crushed chilli.

Avocado bruschetta with Parma ham and poached eggs

This makes a delicious light lunch served with a crisp green salad.

SERVES 4
READY IN 20 MINUTES

4 very fresh eggs
4 thickly cut slices ciabatta loaf
Olive oil, for brushing
1 garlic clove, halved
2 ripe avocados
8 slices Parma ham
Crisp green salad, to serve

1. Preheat the grill to High and bring a shallow pan of water to a gentle simmer. Crack 1 egg into a glass. Swirl the water around with a spoon and drop the egg into the moving water. Add another egg to the pan in the same way. Poach the eggs for 3 minutes for a soft yolk or 5 minutes for a set yolk, then remove with a slotted spoon on to a plate lined with kitchen paper. Cover loosely with foil to keep warm while you poach the other 2 eggs in the same way.

2. Brush the ciabatta slices on both sides with a little oil, and grill until golden and toasted on both sides. Cool slightly, then rub each slice with the garlic halves. Place on 4 serving plates.

3. Halve, stone and peel each avocado, and cut into wedges. Divide among the garlic ciabatta slices and top each with 2 Parma ham slices and a still warm poached egg. Season with salt and pepper, and serve with crisp green salad.

Lancashire and mozzarella cheese sausages with beer gravy and mash

Vegetarians don't have to miss out on the splendour of sausages and mash – this easy recipe is one that everyone can enjoy.

SERVES 6
TAKES 1 HOUR, PLUS CHILLING

400g Lancashire cheese, grated
225g mozzarella, grated
200g fresh white breadcrumbs
6 spring onions, trimmed and
  finely chopped
1 tbsp each chopped fresh
  thyme, basil and parsley leaves
2 medium eggs, plus 3
  medium egg yolks
2 garlic cloves, crushed
Oil, for deep-frying

For the gravy:
3 tbsp vegetable oil
3 large onions, sliced
2 garlic cloves, crushed
1 tbsp light soft brown sugar
25g plain flour
200ml brown ale
500–600ml fresh vegetable
  stock, hot
2 tsp gravy browning or Marmite

For the mash:
1kg floury potatoes, such as
  Maris Piper
150g butter
50g wholegrain mustard

1. Make the sausages. Put all the ingredients except the oil in a large bowl, season well and mix until combined. Divide into 12 and mould each piece into a sausage shape. Cover and chill for 2 hours or overnight.

2. For the gravy, heat the oil in a large heavy-based pan. Add the onions, garlic and sugar, and fry gently for 25–30 minutes until the onions are caramelised. Add the flour and cook for 1 minute. Gradually stir in the ale, stock and gravy browning or Marmite, and bring to the boil. Leave to simmer, stirring occasionally, for 10 minutes. Keep warm.

3. Meanwhile, for the mash, cut the potatoes into large chunks and cook them in boiling salted water for 20 minutes until tender. Drain, tip back into the pan, then season and mash until smooth. Beat in the butter and mustard. Keep warm.

4. Heat some oil for deep-frying to 180°C. Deep-fry the sausages in batches for 3 minutes until richly golden. Remove, drain well on kitchen paper and serve with the mash and gravy.

Feta and spinach free-form pie with tomato relish

This vegetarian pie makes a simple supper, but it would also be ideal served cold at a picnic.

SERVES 4
TAKES 25 MINUTES, PLUS
18–20 MINUTES IN THE OVEN

25g butter, melted
10 sheets fresh filo pastry
200g feta cheese
250g baby leaf spinach
1 tbsp golden raisins
1 tbsp pine nuts
1 garlic clove, crushed
Juice of 1 lemon
200g ricotta, drained

For the tomato relish:

1 tbsp olive oil
1 small onion, finely chopped
1 carrot, finely chopped
1 garlic clove, finely chopped
1 tbsp tomato purée
1 cinnamon stick
200g can chopped tomatoes
75ml vegetable stock

1. Preheat the oven to 190°C/fan 170°C/gas5. Brush a 20cm-round, loose-bottomed tart tin with some of the butter. Lay over a few sheets of filo, slightly overlapping and brush the overhanging filo with more butter. Repeat to use up all the pastry. Set aside.

2. Crumble 125g of the feta into a bowl and mix with the rest of the filling ingredients and some seasoning. Spoon into the filo pastry case and crumble over the remaining feta.

3. Fold the overhanging filo over the filling and scrunch it up roughly to form an edge. Bake for 18–20 minutes until golden and crisp and the filling is piping hot.

4. Meanwhile, make the relish. Heat the oil in a large frying pan over a medium heat. Add the onion, carrot and garlic, and cook, stirring, for 5 minutes. Stir in the purée, cinnamon and tomatoes, and cook for 2–3 minutes. Add the stock and simmer for 8–10 minutes, until reduced slightly. Season to taste. Serve with the filo tart.

Poached eggs Florentine

This classic Italian recipe from Florence is not only tasty but good for you too.

SERVES 4
READY IN 25 MINUTES

65g butter
30g plain flour
300ml milk
1kg fresh spinach, washed
  and any large stalks removed
White wine vinegar, for
  poaching
8 very fresh medium
  free-range eggs
50g Gruyère, coarsely grated
Wholewheat toast, to serve

1. Melt 40g of the butter in a pan, add the flour and cook for 1 minute. Gradually stir in the milk, bring to the boil and leave to simmer gently, stirring occasionally.

2. Pack the spinach into a large pan and cook over a high heat until it has all wilted. Cover and cook for 1 minute. Tip into a colander and press out the liquid. Return to the pan with the remaining butter. Season and keep warm.

3. Preheat the grill to High. Heat 5cm water in a wide, shallow pan until a few bubbles rise up from the base. Add a little vinegar and salt, break in 4 eggs and leave them to poach for 3 minutes. Carefully lift them out on to kitchen paper and repeat with the remaining eggs.

4. Spoon the spinach into 4 buttered ovenproof dishes. Top with the eggs. Stir 40g of the cheese into the sauce, season and spoon over the eggs. Sprinkle over the remaining cheese and grill for 2 minutes, until golden. Serve with wholewheat toast.

Oozy mushroom omelette

A luscious, light and fluffy omelette that tastes very indulgent.

SERVES 4
READY IN 25 MINUTES

4 tbsp olive oil

4 tbsp butter

2 large (about 500g) waxy
potatoes, thinly sliced

250g pack closed cup
mushrooms, thinly sliced

4 garlic cloves, crushed

25g pack fresh chives,
snipped

8 eggs, separated

100g Camembert or Brie,
chopped

1. Heat the oil and 2 tablespoons of the butter in a frying pan over a medium heat. Add the potato slices and cook for 6–8 minutes, until tender and golden brown. Set aside in a bowl.

2. Add the mushrooms to the pan and cook for 3–4 minutes until tender. Add the garlic and cook for 1 minute, then season. Add to the potatoes with most of the chives and toss together.

3. Put the egg whites into a large bowl and whisk into soft peaks. Gently beat the egg yolks and fold them into the egg whites.

4. Melt half the remaining butter in the pan over a high heat. Add half the eggs, lower the heat and cook for 2–3 minutes, until the underside is just set and golden. Sprinkle over half the cheese, potatoes and mushrooms. Flip over the other half of the omelette and slide on to a plate. Repeat with the remaining ingredients.

5. Sprinkle the omelettes with the remaining chives. Halve each one and divide among four warm serving plates to serve.

Variation Replace the garlic and chives with a bunch of finely sliced spring onions, and the Camembert with Cheddar or another hard cheese of your choice.

Smokie haddock pots with Montgomery Cheddar

These are quite rich, so all you really need as an accompaniment is some hot, buttered toast.

SERVES 6–8
TAKES 35 MINUTES, PLUS
20–25 MINUTES IN THE OVEN

800g spinach, washed and
  large stalks removed
1kg undyed smoked haddock
  fillet, skin on
400ml milk
35g unsalted butter
600g tomatoes, halved,
  seeded and sliced
500ml double cream
200g Montgomery or any
  extra-mature cheddar, grated

1. Preheat the oven to 190°C/fan 170°C/gas 5. Put the spinach in a large saucepan and cook over a medium–low heat until the leaves have just wilted. Drain and, when cool, squeeze out the excess liquid. Roughly chop, put into a bowl and season well. Set aside.

2. Put the haddock and milk into a frying pan. Bring just to the boil, cover, and simmer gently for 10 minutes until just cooked. Lift the fish on to a plate and, when cool, flake into pieces, discarding the skin and any bones. Discard the milk.

3. Melt the butter in a frying pan over a high heat, add the tomatoes, and sauté until softened and the cooking juices are reduced. Season and set aside.

4. Arrange the fish, spinach and tomatoes in 6 or 8 x 300ml gratin dishes or 1 x 2.5-litre ovenproof dish, pour over the cream and top with the grated cheese. Bake for 20–25 minutes, until golden and bubbling. Serve immediately.

Creamy pancetta, Brie and mushroom croissants

Croissants don't only have to be eaten for breakfast – you can turn these into a speedy supper on nights when time is tight.

SERVES 2
READY IN 15 MINUTES

25g butter
70g cubed smoked pancetta
1 garlic clove, finely sliced
250g chestnut mushrooms, halved
100ml dry white wine
75ml double cream
Leaves of a few fresh thyme sprigs, plus extra sprigs to garnish
2 freshly baked all-butter croissants.
100g ripe Brie, cut into bite-sized pieces

1. Preheat the grill to High. Melt the butter in a frying pan over a medium heat. Add the smoked pancetta and cook for 3–4 minutes, until golden. Add the garlic and mushrooms, increase the heat and cook for 5–6 minutes, stirring occasionally, until just softened.

2. Add the wine and leave to bubble for a few minutes until it has all evaporated. Reduce the heat, stir in the double cream and thyme leaves, and simmer for a few minutes until thickened. Season to taste.

3. Meanwhile, split open the croissants horizontally and put them on a baking sheet, cut-side up. Grill for 1 minute, until lightly golden. Set the tops aside.

4. Spoon the creamy mushrooms on to each croissant base, scatter with the Brie, and grill for a further 2 minutes, until the cheese is melting. Cover with the tops and serve hot, scattered with the extra thyme sprigs.

Tomato and spicy sausage baked eggs with cornbread

These eggs are baked in a spicy tomato sauce, and the cornbread is ideal for mopping up all the juices.

SERVES 4

TAKES 45 MINUTES, PLUS
ABOUT 30 MINUTES IN THE OVEN

2 tbsp olive oil

1 large red onion, roughly chopped

150g spicy chorizo, roughly chopped

1 red pepper, seeded and chopped

2 x 400g cans chopped tomatoes

4 large eggs

½ mild green chilli, seeded and chopped, to serve (optional)

For the cornbread:

40g butter, melted, plus extra for greasing

200g plain flour

150g cornmeal

2 tsp baking powder

2 green chillies, seeded and finely chopped

2 tbsp mature Cheddar, grated

2 large eggs

150ml milk

1. Make the cornbread. Preheat the oven to 200°C/fan 180°C/gas 6. Grease a 16cm x 25cm shallow non-stick roasting tin. Mix the flour, cornmeal, baking powder, chillies, cheese and a pinch of salt together in a large bowl. Beat the eggs, milk and the 40g of melted butter in another bowl and mix into the dry ingredients. Pour into the tin and bake for 25–30 minutes, until golden and cooked through.

2. Meanwhile, heat the oil in a large ovenproof frying pan and fry the onion for 5 minutes, until softened. Stir in the chorizo and cook for 3–4 minutes. Stir in the red pepper, tomatoes and 100ml of water. Simmer for 12–15 minutes, until the pepper is soft and the mixture is thickened. Season.

3. Make four wells in the mixture. Crack in the eggs, transfer the pan to the oven and bake for 3–4 minutes or until the eggs are set. Garnish with the chilli, if using, and serve with hunks of the cornbread.

Variation Use canned ratatouille in place of the canned tomatoes for a change.

Cheese and ham rice cakes

These are ideal to prepare ahead – do so and supper could be on the table in less than 20 minutes.

MAKES 12

TAKES 40 MINUTES, PLUS
10–15 MINUTES IN THE OVEN,
PLUS SETTING AND COOLING

1 tbsp olive oil
Large knob of butter
1 onion, finely chopped
1 large garlic clove, crushed
300g risotto rice
1.3 litres chicken stock, hot
4 slices cooked ham, cubed
100g mozzarella, cut into
  small cubes
Handful of fresh flatleaf parsley,
  finely chopped
3 large free-range eggs
100g plain flour
100g dried breadcrumbs
Crispy green salad, to serve

1. Heat the oil and butter in a pan, add the onion and cook gently for 4–5 minutes. Add the garlic and rice, and stir well.

2. Add enough stock just to cover the rice, season and simmer gently, stirring, until the stock has been absorbed. Repeat until all the stock has been used and the rice is tender and creamy – this should take about 20–25 minutes – then set aside to cool.

3. Add the ham, mozzarella, parsley and 1 egg to the cooled rice and mix well. Using wet hands, shape the mixture into 12 balls, then flatten into discs. Put on a non-stick baking sheet, cover with cling film and chill for at least 20 minutes.

4. When ready to cook, preheat the oven to 200°C/fan 180°C/gas 6. Beat the remaining eggs in a shallow dish. In two other shallow dishes, place the flour and breadcrumbs. Coat the cakes in the flour, then the egg, then the breadcrumbs. Return to the baking sheet and bake for 10–15 minutes, until golden. Serve with a crispy green salad.

★ DELICIOUS. TIP These simple rice cakes are an excellent way of using up leftover risotto.

Ham, roasted red pepper and goat's cheese pizza

Homemade pizzas take more time to make, but they taste so much better, especially when they use such lovely ingredients.

serves 8
takes about 50 minutes, plus 15 minutes in the oven, plus rising and cooling

3 tbsp olive oil, plus extra for greasing
2 garlic cloves, crushed
3 x 400g cans chopped tomatoes
½ tsp sugar
1 tbsp chopped fresh oregano
10 slices San Daniele ham
2 roasted red peppers from a jar, drained and cut into strips
2 x 75g small rinded goat's cheeses, thinly sliced
150g Parmesan cheese shavings, plus extra for serving
Small fresh basil leaves, to garnish

For the base:

400g strong white flour, plus extra for dusting
1 tbsp easy-blend dried yeast
1½ tsp salt
1 tbsp olive oil, plus extra for greasing

1. For the base, sift the flour, yeast and salt into a bowl. Add the oil and 250–260ml hand-hot water, and mix to a soft dough. Turn out and knead until smooth. Return to a lightly oiled bowl, cover and leave somewhere warm for 1 hour, or until doubled in size.

2. Meanwhile, heat the oil and garlic in a large frying pan, add the tomatoes and sugar, and simmer for 20–25 minutes, until thick. Stir in the oregano and season.

3. Preheat the oven to 240°C/fan 220°C/gas 9. Lightly oil 2 Swiss roll tins (about 23cm x 33cm), then line with baking paper. Punch down the dough, knead once more until smooth, then cut in half. Roll each piece out and use to line the base and sides of each tin. Spread over the tomato sauce.

4. Tear the ham into large pieces. Arrange over the top of each pizza with the red peppers, goat's cheese and cheese shavings. Bake for 15 minutes or until golden brown. Slide on to a board and cut into 8 pieces. Shave over more cheese and scatter with the basil leaves.

Cheese and thyme soufflés

There's no need for any special dishes for these soufflés, as they can be baked in any individual shallow ovenproof dishes – even soup plates would do.

SERVES 4

TAKES 10 MINUTES, PLUS
15–16 MINUTES IN THE OVEN,
PLUS OVERNIGHT DRAINING

25g butter, melted

150g Parmesan or Grana
  Padano, finely grated

4 large very fresh eggs

250g ricotta (drained overnight
  in a sieve if from a tub)

100ml double cream

1 tsp fresh thyme leaves, plus
  extra to garnish

Dressed mixed leaf salad,
  to serve

1. Preheat the oven to 200°C/fan 180°C/gas 6. Grease 4 x 250ml shallow, oval ovenproof dishes with the melted butter. Sprinkle the insides with 25g of the cheese.

2. Separate the eggs into 2 large mixing bowls. Lightly beat the egg yolks until smooth, then whisk in the ricotta. Stir in the cream and thyme leaves, then fold in 75g of the grated cheese and season.

3. Whisk the egg whites to soft peaks, then gently fold into the cheese mixture. Divide the mixture among the dishes and sprinkle with the extra thyme leaves and the remaining grated cheese.

4. Place the dishes on a baking sheet and bake in the oven for 15–16 minutes, or until well risen and golden. Serve immediately with a dressed mixed leaf salad.

How to take the stress out of cooking every day

For many of us, eating home-cooked food every day is something that we all want to do, but the pressures of modern living and busy weekdays can take the pleasure out of it. Over the next few pages there are some top tips on how you can make your life a little easier and make home-cooked food less of a chore.

PLANNING AHEAD

All you need is a little thought and some forward planning and you can make shopping for, preparing, cooking and eating interesting foods a whole lot easier.

• Keep your storecupboard, fridge and freezer well stocked with basic non-perishable ingredients (see pages 183–5).

• Set aside a little time each week to plan your food and shopping for the coming week. Just 1 hour of constructive thinking will save you the time and stress of having to decide what to cook for dinner as you get home at the end of a busy day.

• If you plan on entertaining mid-week, cook something very simple, for which you only have to buy one or two fresh ingredients at the most on the day. If you can, cook something in advance and freeze or chill it for reheating on the night.

SHOPPING

• Check through your storecupboard, fridge, vegetable and fruit basket and freezer from time to time. Turf out anything that's past its sell-by date: although it is probably still edible, it will often have lost the best of its flavour.

• Think about your food for the week ahead; with careful shopping, you should quite easily be able to make it through to the following weekend with maybe a quick shop for some fresh salads, vegetables or fruit once or twice. Fish, however, is best eaten on the day you buy it.

• Keep an on-going shopping list in the kitchen so that you don't forget what it was you needed when you come to make your list. As things run out, jot them down, then expand on the list just before you go shopping. Trawling up and down the aisles racking your brains as to what you need is frustrating and a waste of time. You could even break up your list into obvious sections – such as fruit and vegetables, storecupboard staples, dairy goods, things from the chiller cabinet and fresh produce such as meat and fish. Supermarkets are divided into these sections too, and it's quicker to deal with one at a time, instead of shuttling backwards and forwards from one section to another.

• Try not to buy too much at any one time, or you may not have space to store the non-perishable stuff – or perishable goods – which might go off before you've had the chance to eat them. Buy fresh produce little and often, or as often as you can, and make one 'big shop' to the supermarket each week to keep the storecupboard, fridge and freezer well stocked.

A SHOPPING CHECKLIST

With a good supply of basic foodstuffs in the storecupboard or fridge, you can always rustle something up at short notice, and lessen the amount of stuff to buy when you fancy cooking something different. Good things to have on stand-by are:

In the storecupboard:

Cans	Chopped tomatoes (large and small)
	Naturally sweet sweetcorn kernels
	Chickpeas, red kidney beans and white beans such as cannellini or butter beans
	Tuna – in olive oil, sunflower oil or spring water
	Coconut milk
	Small cans of evaporated milk
Oils	Sunflower, ordinary olive, a good extra virgin olive oil and toasted sesame oil
Vinegars	Red, white wine and balsamic

A good-quality vegetable stock powder or cube, such as Marigold Stock – chicken, vegetable and beef

Basmati rice, long grain rice, risotto rice (such as arborio) and pudding rice
Couscous
Dried red and Puy lentils
A selection of dried pasta shapes – macaroni, penne, spaghetti and tagliatelle
Rolled porridge oats
Cornmeal or polenta
Plain, self-raising and wholemeal flour
Cornflour
Baking powder
Sugar – caster, demerara, light soft brown or light muscovado and icing

Buy these regularly, in small amounts, and keep a watchful eye on the sell-by date. Grinding whole spices just before you use them is always the best option, but fresh ready-ground spices are fine, as long as they are fresh.

The most useful ones to have are: cooking salt and sea salt flakes, black peppercorns, cumin seed and powder, coriander seed and powder, green cardamom pods, cloves, cinnamon sticks, ground turmeric, garam masala powder, cayenne pepper, chilli powder, paprika, dried crushed chillies, black mustard seeds, whole nutmegs, dried oregano and a bottle of vanilla extract

Runny honey, jam, marmalade, maple syrup, Dijon and wholegrain mustard, a mild or medium-hot curry paste and mango chutney

Dark soy sauce, tomato ketchup, brown sauce,
Worcestershire sauce, tomato passata (sieved
tomatoes) and small cartons of coconut cream

Onions
Potatoes
Garlic
Fresh root ginger
A few lemons

Milk
Orange or apple juice
½ dozen eggs
Butter
Lard
Natural yogurt
Jars of prepared ginger and garlic (these products,
although not as fresh tasting as the real thing, cut
down enormously on the preparation time and are
a great stand-by)
Tomato purée, in a tube
A piece of Cheddar and a wedge of Parmesan
A jar of mayonnaise

Bread – including pitta, naan and chapatis
Ice cubes
Frozen peas and leaf spinach
Milk
Homemade stock
Vanilla ice cream
A block of puff pastry

Freezing

You don't have to use your freezer just for storing lots of uncooked ingredients, such as meat and fish. You could also use it as a supply of emergency foods – a few leftovers and a few basics. In addition to the food listed on pages 183–5, why not keep a Margherita pizza in there, too, to which you can add a few extra toppings, or tubs of homemade soup for lunches (which you can make in a large batch and freeze in single portions). It is also handy to make a batch of bolognese sauce which you can use for pasta or lasagne, and stock, which you can freeze in 300ml pots.

● When freezing any foods, whether homemade or bought, always label the container with the date and the year – it's scary how time can slip by. There is a misconception that you can store food in a freezer for ever – this is definitely not the case, as you will discover should you ever thaw out and try to eat something that has been in there far too long. Freezing merely slows down the deterioration of food – it does not preserve it for ever – and in the end the continuous presence of ice in the food breaks down its structure and makes it unpalatable.

● Make sure you pack things adequately to protect them. If they are exposed to the cold, ice and air, they will dry out and go white, which is known as 'freezer burn'. The food is then ruined. The package needs to be air-tight. Plastic freezer bags are designed specifically for this purpose: they are stronger and protect the food better. When sealing something in a plastic bag for freezing, try to remove as much air as possible and then seal it well. Small, stackable plastic boxes are ideal for portions of soup, pasta sauces, casseroles and curries.

● Allow home-cooked foods to cool down to room temperature before freezing them.

● Be aware of the star system on ready-made products. Domestic freezers and frozen-food compartments of a fridge have different star ratings according to the temperature at which they operate. This determines how long certain products can be stored in them, together with the best-before date on the packet.

*   a frozen-food compartment with a temp of -6°C
Store up to 1 week

**   a frozen-food compartment with a temp of -12°C
Store up to 1 month

***   a frozen-food compartment with a temp of -18°C
Store until best-before date

**** a food freezer with a temp of -18°C or colder
Store until best-before date

• Here is a rough guide to the maximum storage time for certain foods stored at -18°C:

4 months: fish, sausages, ready meals, cakes and pastries

6 months: meat and poultry

8 months: vegetables and fruit

• Try to get frozen food for the freezer home as soon as possible. If necessary, and especially in warm weather, take lots of newspapers or even a cool box with you so that it can't thaw out on the way home. You could also stick your freezer on 'Fast Freeze' for a few hours once you place the food in the freezer. (This is particularly worth doing with non-frozen foods for the freezer.)

• Never re-freeze thawed frozen foods, as you can stand the risk of food poisoning.

• Do not overcrowd the freezer. Your freezer manual will tell you its maximum capacity.

• Once thawed, frozen foods become as perishable as fresh, so use them straight away.

• Defrost and clean out your freezer at least 3 times a year. As it ices up it begins to work less efficiently, shortening the safe storage time of your food, and lots of ice takes up lots of useful space.

Index

apricot and turkey burgers with
    sweet potato wedges 84–5
artichokes 20, 156
    roasted and pancetta pasta
        12–13
aubergine
    and chestnut tagine with herb
        couscous 134–5
    and tomato and mozzarella
        gratin 148–9
avocado
    bruschetta with Parma ham
        and poached eggs 160–1
    pesto with spaghetti 24–5

bacon 156
    and leek and herb stuffing
        with roast chicken 90–1
    and liver with celeriac mash
        50–1
barley, pearl risotto with roasted
    squash, red peppers and
    rocket 38–9
basil
    and macaroni and pancetta
        frittata 20–1
    and lemon and olive butter
        with salmon steaks 104–5
    and tomato potatoes, roast
        with Parmesan turkey 76–7
beans 18, 156
    pesto and tomato and caper
        salsa with tuna 120–1
beef 62
    and bok choi noodles 32–3
    Mexican minced and spicy
        polenta cobbler 58–9
    steak tagliata with roasted
        vine tomatoes 60–2
    stuffed rolls with tomato and
        olive sauce 48–9
beer gravy with Lancashire and
    mozzarella cheese sausages
    and mash 162–3

biryani
    lamb 14–15
    vegetable 152–3
bok choi and beef noodles 32–3
bread and butter bake, Stilton
    and leek 136–7
broccoli, purple sprouting 32
bruschetta, avocado with Parma
    ham and poached eggs
    160–1
burgers, turkey and apricot with
    sweet potato wedges 84–5
butter, basil, lemon and olive
    with salmon steaks 104–5

caper and tomato salsa and
    pesto beans with tuna 120–1
cauliflower and macaroni cheese
    138–9
celeriac mash with liver and
    bacon 50–1
cheese see also individual
        entries
    Brie and pancetta and
        mushroom croissants,
        creamy 172–3
    Camembert 168
    Cheddar 138, 168, 174
    cream cheese and salmon
        gnocchi 106–7
    creamy blue and butternut
        squash risotto 22–3
    Emmental 42
    Grana Padano 60, 180
    Gruyère 42, 146
    and ham rice cakes 176–7
    Montgomery Cheddar with
        smokie haddock pots 170–1
    and thyme soufflés 180–1
chestnut and aubergine tagine
    with herb couscous 134–5
chicken 30, 32, 74, 76, 132
    and chorizo pilaff 72–3
    coq au vin, cheat's 82–3

with honey and mustard glaze
    88–9
Mediterranean stuffed 78–9
poussin, chorizo and wild and
    red rice-stuffed 94–5
roast with bacon, leek and
    herb stuffing 90–1
rosemary and honey roast
    with garlic mash 70–1
and spinach curry 80–1
and vegetable noodles,
    stir-fried 92–3
chilli
    and prawns, lemon, garlic and
        rocket with spaghetti 16–17
    prawns, sweet and sour
        110–11
chorizo
    and chicken pilaff 72–3
    with mussels 108–9
    and prawn jambalaya 30–1
    and tomato baked eggs with
        cornbread 174–5
    and wild and red rice-stuffed
        poussin 94–5
cider 108
coconut batter, cod goujons in
    114–15
cod, chunky goujons in coconut
    batter 114–15
cornbread with tomato and spicy
    sausage baked eggs 174–5
couscous
    herb with aubergine and
        chestnut tagine 134–5
    spring vegetable 36–7
crème fraîche and tomato and
    red onion tart 130–1
crêpe bake, spinach and
    mushroom 146–7
croissants, pancetta, Brie and
    mushroom, creamy 172–3
cumin raita with Indian spiced
    pork koftas 62–3

curry
  chicken and spinach 80–1
  egg, Anglo-Indian 158–9
  fish 116–17
  green Thai with greens
    128–9
  Thai duck, aromatic 86–7
  vegetable 144–5
curry powder, Madras-style 62

dill and salmon and spinach
  potato bake 100–1
dressing, sundried tomato with
  roasted squash and red
  pepper salad 142–3
duck
  five spice and ginger noodle
    soup 26–7
  honeyed and vegetable stir-fry
    74–5
  Thai curry, aromatic 86–7
dumplings, herb with vegetable
  stew 132–3

eggs 176
  Anglo-Indian curry 158–9
  baked and tomato and spicy
    sausage with cornbread
    174–5
  hard-boiled 152
  poached with avocado
    bruschetta and Parma ham
    160–1
  poached Florentine 166–7

fennel and lamb and orange
  spring stew, quick 54–5
feta cheese 20
  and spinach free-form pie
    with tomato relish 164–5
fish 76, 96–125
  baked with herb crust and
    tartare sauce 98–9
  curry 116–17
  pie 118–1
fishcakes, smoked haddock with
  horseradish mayo 122–3

five-spice duck and ginger
  noodle soup 26–7
freezing 186–7
frittata
  macaroni, pancetta and basil
    20–1
  spicy salami, roasted pepper
    and taleggio 156–7

gammon steaks, grilled with
  caramelised black pepper
  pineapple 46–7
garlic
  mash with rosemary and
    honey roast chicken 70–1
  and prawns, lemon, chilli
    and rocket with spaghetti
    16–17
  and saffron and paprika
    seafood stew 112–13
ginger and five spice duck
  noodle soup 26–7
gnocchi
  salmon and cream cheese
    106–7
  with Tuscan sausage and
    porcini sauce 34–5
goat's cheese 22, 78
  and ham and roasted red
    pepper pizza 178–9
gratin, aubergine, tomato and
  mozzarella 148–9
greens with green Thai curry
  128–9

haddock, smoked
  fishcakes with horseradish
    mayo 122–3
  pots with Montgomery
    Cheddar 170–1
ham
  and cheese rice cakes 176–7
  hock and split pea and mint
    stew 52–3
  Parma 156; with avocado
    bruschetta and poached
    eggs 160–1

and roasted red pepper and
  goat's cheese pizza 178–9
herbs
  and bacon and leek stuffing
    with roast chicken 90–1
  crust on baked fish with
    tartare sauce 98–9
  couscous with aubergine and
    chestnut tagine 134–5
  dumplings with vegetable
    stew 132–3
honey
  and mustard glaze with
    chicken 88–9
  and rosemary roast chicken
    with garlic mash 70–1
honeyed duck and vegetable
  stir-fry 74–5
horseradish mayo with smoked
  haddock fishcakes 122–3

Indian pickles 14
Indian spiced pork koftas with
  cumin raita 62–3

jambalaya, prawn and chorizo
  30–1

koftas, Indian spiced pork with
  cumin raita 62–3

laksa, prawn, easy 28–9
lamb 62
  biryani 14–15
  chops, devilled 64–5
  farmers' mince 44–5
  and orange and fennel spring
    stew, quick 54–5
Lancashire and mozzarella
  cheese sausages with beer
  gravy and mash 162–3
leeks
  and bacon and herb stuffing
    with roast chicken 90–1
  and Stilton bread and butter
    bake 136–7
lemon 158

and basil and olive butter with salmon steaks 104–5

and prawns, chilli, garlic and rocket with spaghetti 16–17

lemon sole, deep-fried with green mayonnaise 124–5

liver and bacon with celeriac mash 50–1

macaroni
and cauliflower cheese 138–9
and pancetta and basil frittata 20–1

maple syrup 70

mash
with beer gravy and Lancashire and mozzarella sausages 162–3
celeriac with liver and bacon 50–1
garlic with rosemary and honey roast chicken 70–1

mayonnaise
green with deep-fried lemon sole 124–5
horseradish with smoked haddock fishcakes 122–3

meat 40–67

Mediterranean stuffed chicken 78–9

Mexican minced beef with spicy polenta cobbler 58–9

mint and ham hock and split pea stew 52–3

mozzarella 176
and aubergine and tomato gratin 148–9
and Lancashire sausages with beer gravy and mash 162–3

mushrooms
omelette, oozy 168–9
and pancetta and Brie croissants, creamy 172–3
porcini sauce and sausage, Tuscan with gnocchi 34–5
portabello 22
and spinach crêpe bake 146–7

and taleggio pastry melt 150–1

mussels with chorizo 108–9

mustard and honey glaze with chicken 88–9

naan bread 14, 80
pizzas 66–7

noodles
beef and bok choi 32–3
chicken and vegetable, stir-fried 92–3
and five spice duck and ginger soup 26–7

nutmeg 146

olives
and basil and lemon butter with salmon steaks 104–5
and tomato sauce with stuffed beef rolls 48–9

omelette, oozy mushroom 168–9

onion, red and tomato and crème fraîche tart 130–1

onions, spring 168

orange and lamb and fennel spring stew, quick 54–5

pak choi 32

pancetta
and Brie and mushroom croissants, creamy 172–3
and macaroni and basil frittata 20–1
and roasted artichoke pasta 12–13

paprika 72
and saffron and garlic seafood stew 112–13

Parmesan cheese 22, 34, 44, 60, 118, 120, 138, 140, 178, 180
turkey with roast tomato and basil potatoes 76–7

parsnips 44

pasta, roasted artichoke and pancetta 12–13

pastry

puff 150, 185
shortcrust 130

pastry melt, taleggio and mushroom 150–1

peas 20, 156
split pea and ham hock and mint stew 52–3

peppers, red 20
roasted and goat's cheese and ham pizza 178–9
roasted and spicy salami and taleggio frittata 156–7
and roasted squash and rocket with pearl barley risotto 38–9
and roasted squash salad with sundried tomato dressing 142–3

pesto
avocado with spaghetti 24–5
beans and tomato and caper salsa with tuna 20–1

pies
feta and spinach, free-form with tomato relish 164–5
fish 118–19

pilaff, chicken and chorizo 72–3

pineapple, black pepper, caramelised with grilled gammon steaks 46–7

pizzas
ham, roasted red pepper and goat's cheese 178–9
naan bread 66–7

polenta cobbler, spicy and Mexican minced beef 58–9

pork 32
grilled chops, rarebit-style 42–3
Indian spiced koftas with cumin raita 62–3

potatoes
bake, salmon, spinach and dill 100–1
mash with Lancashire and mozzarella cheese

sausages and beer gravy 162–3
tomato and basil, roast with Parmesan turkey 76–7
poultry 68–95
prawns 72, 146
chilli, sweet and sour 110–11
and chorizo jambalaya 30–1
laksa, easy 28–9
and lemon, chilli, garlic and rocket with spaghetti 16–17

raita, cumin with Indian spiced pork koftas 62–3
ratatouille 174
rice
cakes, cheese and ham 176–7
dirty, paella-style 18–19
wild and red and chorizo-stuffed poussin 94–5
risotto
butternut squash and creamy blue cheese 22–3
pearl barley with roasted squash, red peppers and rocket 38–9
rocket
and prawns, lemon, chilli and garlic with spaghetti 16–17
and roasted squash and red peppers with pearl barley risotto 38–9
rosemary and honey roast chicken with garlic mash 70–1

saffron 72
and paprika and garlic seafood stew 112–13
salad 64, 94, 98, 124, 150, 160, 176, 180
Niçoise 102–3
roasted squash and red pepper with sundried tomato dressing 142–3
watercress 46
salami, spicy and roasted pepper

and taleggio frittata 156–7
salmon 146
and cream cheese gnocchi 106–7
and spinach and dill potato bake 100–1
steaks with basil, lemon and olive butter 104–5
salsa, tomato and caper with tuna and pesto beans 120–1
sauces 92, 146
porcini and sausage 34–5
tartare 98–9
tomato and olive 48–9
sausages 56, 136 see also chorizo
Lancashire and mozzarella cheese with beer gravy and mash 162–3
and porcini sauce, Tuscan with gnocchi 34–5
Sicilian with roasted sweet potatoes 56–7
spicy and tomato baked eggs with cornbread 174–5
shopping 182–5
Sicilian sausages with roasted sweet potatoes 56–7
soufflés, cheese and thyme 180–1
soups
five spice duck and ginger noodle 26–7
mulligatawny 80
prawn laksa, easy 28–9
spaghetti
with avocado pesto 24–5
with prawns, lemon, chilli, garlic and rocket 16–17
spinach 46, 158
and chicken curry 80–1
and feta free-form pie with tomato relish 164–5
and mushroom crêpe bake 146–7
and paprika and garlic seafood stew 112–13

poached eggs Florentine 166–7
and salmon and dill potato bake 100–1
squash 56, 156
butternut and creamy blue cheese risotto 22–3
and red peppers, roasted with pearl barley risotto and rocket 38–9
and red pepper, roasted salad with sundried tomato dressing 142–3
stews
saffron, paprika and garlic seafood stew 112–13
ham hock, split pea and mint 52–3
lamb, orange and fennel spring, quick 54–5
vegetable with herb dumplings 132–3
Stilton and leek bread and butter bake 136–7
stir-fry
chicken and vegetable noodles 92–3
honeyed duck and vegetable 74–5
storecupboard 183–5
stuffing
bacon, leek and herb 90–1
chorizo and wild and red rice 94–5
Mediterranean 78–9
sweet potatoes
roasted with Sicilian sausages 56–7
wedges with turkey and apricot burgers 84–5
Swiss chard 46

tagine, aubergine and chestnut with herb couscous 134–5
taleggio
and mushroom pastry melt 150–1

and spicy salami and roasted pepper frittata 156–7

tart, tomato, red onion and crème fraîche 130–1

tartare sauce with baked fish in herb crust 98–9

Thai curry, green with greens 128–9

Thai duck curry, aromatic 86–7

thyme 22, 70, 78, 138, 172
and cheese soufflés 180–1

tomatoes 78
and aubergine and mozzarella gratin 148–9
baked stuffed 140–1
and basil potatoes, roast with Parmesan turkey 76–7
and caper salsa and pesto beans with tuna 120–1

and olive sauce with stuffed beef rolls 48–9

and red onion and crème fraîche tart 130–1

relish with feta and spinach free-form pie 164–5

and spicy sausage baked eggs with cornbread 174–5

sundried dressing with roasted squash and red pepper salad 142–3

vin, roasted with steak tagliata 60–1

toppings 44, 98

tuna with tomato and caper salsa and pesto beans 120–1

turkey
and apricot burgers with sweet potato wedges 84–5

Parmesan with roast tomato and basil potatoes 76–7

Tuscan sausage and porcini sauce with gnocchi 34–5

vegetables
biryani 152–3
and chicken noodles, stir-fried 92–3
curry 144–5
and honeyed duck stir-fry 74–5
spring couscous 36–7
stew with herb dumplings 132–3

watercress salad 46

yogurt 14

Picture and recipe credits

Harper Collins would like to thank the following for providing photographs:

Steve Baxter p25, p33, p35, p39, p65, p67, p71, p91, p101, p119, p121, p123, p125, p129, p135, p141, p143, p145, p149, p161, p163, p167, p179, p181; Peter Cassidy p23, p61, p111; Jean Cazals p45; Jonathan Gregson p21, p27, p29, p31, p95, p159; Janine Hosegood p105; Richard Jung p55, p57, p109, p171; Gareth Morgans p79; Lis Parsons p51, p59, p63, p73, p75, p77, p85, p87, p107, p117, p147, p151, p173; Michael Paul p43, p47, p89, p99, p103; Craig Robertson p13, p15,

p19, p53, p137, p153, p157, p165, p169, p175, p177; Lucinda Symons p49, p133; Peter Thiedeke p81, p83; Philip Webb p17, p113, p115, p139; Rob White p37, p131

With thanks, too, for the following for creating the recipes for delicious. which are used in this book:

Kate Belcher p14, p24, p30, p74, p76, p78, p80, p100, p130, p152, p160, p172; Angela Boggiano p12, p92, p94, p138, p156, p176; Angela Boggiano and Kate Belcher p52; Angela Boggiano and Alice Hart p168, p174; Adrian Daniel p134;

Matthew Drennan p104, p118; Silvana Franco p20, p50, p54, p56, p136; Brian Glover p88; Diana Henry p108, p170; Catherine Hill p34, p70, p82, p150; Debbie Major p16, p26, p32, p38, p42, p46, p58, p60, p86, p90, p98, p110, p112, p114, p120, p124, p140, p142, p148, p166, p178, p180; Kim Morphew p106; Tom Norrington-Davies p28, p36, p64, p102, p144, p158; Simon Rimmer p18, p116, p128, p162, p164; Carol Tennant p48, p132; Linda Tubby p22; Jenny White p72, p122, p146; Lucy Williams p66; Mitzie Wilson p44, p62, p84